The Open University

Block 1

France, England and Burgundy in the fifteenth century

Kathleen Daly and Rosemary O'Day

This publication forms part of an Open University course *A200 Exploring History: Medieval to Modern 1400–1900*. Details of this and other Open University courses can be obtained from the Student Registration and Enquiry Service, The Open University, PO Box 197, Milton Keynes, MK7 6BJ, United Kingdom: tel. +44 (0)870 333 4340, email general-enquiries@open.ac.uk

Alternatively, you may visit the Open University website at http://www.open.ac.uk where you can learn more about the wide range of courses and packs offered at all levels by The Open University.

To purchase a selection of Open University course materials visit http://www.ouw.co.uk, or contact Open University Worldwide, Michael Young Building, Walton Hall, Milton Keynes MK7 6AA, United Kingdom for a brochure, tel. +44 (0)1908 858785; fax +44 (0)1908 858787; email ouwenq@open.ac.uk

The Open University
Walton Hall, Milton Keynes
MK7 6AA

First published 2007

Edited and designed by The Open University.

Typeset by The Open University

Printed in Great Britain by Bell & Bain Ltd., Glasgow

ISBN 978 0 7492 17143

2.1

B/a200_B1_e1i2_N9780749216825

Mixed Sources
Product group from well-managed forests and other controlled sources
www.fsc.org Cert no. TT-COC-002769
© 1996 Forest Stewardship Council

FSC

The paper used in this publication contains pulp sourced from forests independently certified to the Forest Stewardship Council (FSC) principles and criteria. Chain of custody certification allows the pulp from these forests to be tracked to the end use (see www.fsc-uk.org).

CONTENTS

INTRODUCTION

Kathleen Daly

WHAT YOU NEED TO STUDY THIS BLOCK

- Units 1–4
- *Course Guide*
- *Media Guide*
- *Visual Sources*
- Set book: Wallace, P.G. (ed.) (2004) *The Long European Reformation: Religion, Political Conflict and the Search for Conformity, 1350–1750*, London, Palgrave Macmillan
- Anthology documents
- Secondary sources on the course website
- Images from the Beauchamp Pageant Book provided electronically with the secondary sources
- DVD 1
- TMA 01

Learning outcomes

When you have finished this block you should be able to:

- understand and discuss aspects of the ideology and exercise of power in England, France and Burgundy, and the extent to which the term 'state' can be applied to these principalities.

- understand aspects of the links between power and consumption, particularly in Burgundy.

- read and analyse primary sources of several kinds, including visual sources as well as written texts, in the context of the three themes of the block: the formation of the state; producers and consumers; and beliefs and ideologies (you will use a DVD to help with this outcome)

- read and use appropriately a secondary source (from a historical work written for students).

INTRODUCTION TO THE THEMES OF THE BLOCK

I would like to introduce the themes of this block by discussing one of my favourite medieval miniatures: 'The legend of the fleurs de lis' from the *Bedford Book of Hours* (see *Visual Sources*, Plate I.1).

On one level, this is a simple illustration of the legend of the conversion of Clovis, the first Christian king who, in the late fifth and early sixth centuries, ruled part of what would later become France. His wife, a Burgundian princess who became St Clothilda, had already begged her pagan husband to convert, but without success. On the eve of Clovis's battle, Clothilda handed him a coat of arms with three lilies on it, which had been given to her by a hermit who had miraculously received it from an angel. Clovis took the new arms, converted to Christianity and then defeated his pagan rival. The lilies became the royal coat of arms.

Once we know more about the book, however, we can understand this picture better. The book was originally made in Paris for John, duke of Bedford and regent of France, probably when he married Anne of Burgundy (in 1423), sister of Philip the Good, duke of Burgundy. The marriage was extremely important diplomatically. As regent, Bedford ruled France on behalf of his tiny nephew Henry VI, who was then in England (of which he was also king). Philip of Burgundy was a key English ally, and this marriage forged a family bond between Bedford and Burgundy (see Figure I.1). However, this particular illustration was not part of the original book, but was added in about 1430. The date is important: Henry VI was just about to be crowned king of France and Anne presented him with this book a few weeks before the ceremony, when he was staying with her and her husband in Normandy (Backhouse, 1990, pp. 56–61).

This knowledge leads us to different levels of interpretation. On one level, this picture seems to justify Henry's rightful claim to rule France, as a descendant of the French as well as the English royal house. On another, Anne appears to be reminding the king of the kingdom of France's debt to a Burgundian princess, like her, and of Henry's own inheritance of the divinely protected French crown. On yet another, it illustrates the close association between religious beliefs and what we would call politics. Henry VI believed that his power came from God, by whose permission he claimed to be the 'very Christian king' of France, even though, in practice, almost all the kingdom south of the river Loire acknowledged not Henry but his uncle Charles VII (who claimed all the same privileges).

But the context for all this interpretation is a material object. The illustration is part of a book of hours – essentially a collection of prayers, readings and often pictures used in private religious devotion by the laity. The Bedford Hours was a costly, precious object, illustrated by a leading Parisian artist known as the Bedford Master and his associates. It is therefore an example of consumption, by a princely patron, of the product of a skilled craftsman. What is more, it was made at a time that is generally recognised as one of economic crisis,

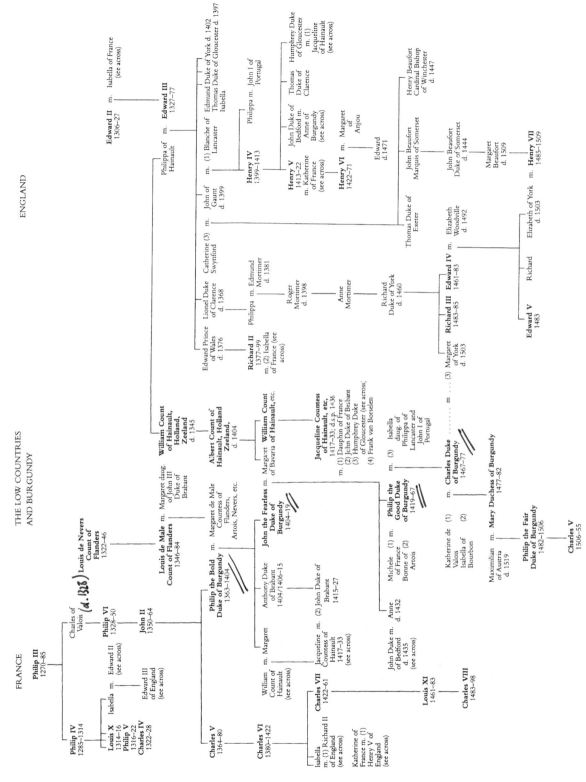

The Ruling Dynasties of France, the Low Countries, Burgundy and England 1300–1500

Figure I.1 The genealogies of France, Burgundy and England, adapted from Caroline Barron and Nigel Saul (1995) *England and the Low Countries in the Late Middle Ages*, Stroud, Alan Sutton Publishing Ltd/New York, St Martin's Press

when Paris in particular had been badly affected by a drop in population and its economy had been damaged by years of civil war and foreign invasion. Knowing this may in itself raise questions. Was this image intended just for Henry to look at when he was saying his prayers? Or was it part of a much broader movement to try to convince the French that Henry was their legitimate king?

These complex questions bring us to the three themes we shall be exploring in the block: the formation of the state; producers and consumers; and beliefs and ideologies.

What do we understand by the 'medieval state'? In some respects it was so unlike what we associate with modern – particularly western – states that some historians have even refused to recognise medieval principalities as states at all. For example, a modern state is usually characterised by:

* sovereignty over a particular territory
* extensive military, financial, judicial and administrative powers
* a large administration in the service of the state
* some sense of common identity between the inhabitants of a particular country.

These weren't the major features of a medieval state. In this block, we shall consider the extent to which the term 'state' can be applied to England, France and Burgundy. In looking at the 'formation of the state', we shall consider how medieval rulers and their subjects reacted and adapted to changing conditions. We shall try to understand how and why powers that are familiar to us today developed during the fifteenth century, and also how and why another whole range of beliefs and structures that are unfamiliar to us had their part to play in medieval government. In Unit 2, in particular, we shall also consider how the production of cultural artefacts – including books – can enrich our understanding of the interplay between power and consumption.

In the first three units, but particularly in Unit 3, we shall look at the context of government against the background of a greatly reduced population (the outbreak of Black Death in 1348 had caused the population to fall by as much as one-third), and against the uncertainties of war and economic fluctuations. In all units, but particularly in Unit 4, we shall consider religious beliefs and practices.

Throughout the block, we shall consider a range of visual and textual evidence which, like the *Bedford Book of Hours*, can deepen our historical understanding – and, we hope, enjoyment – of the period we are studying. We shall also use a DVD to explore a medieval mansion, a tomb and some parish churches. While exploring how historians can use buildings and objects as evidence, we hope to illuminate some of the key themes of the course, such as the ways in which wealth was spent, and how complex ideas and beliefs about religion and the state could be conveyed through imagery.

We hope that you will enjoy working through this block. Much of the material may be unfamiliar to you, but please do not worry – in the words of the fifteenth-century 'civil servant' and historian Mathieu Thomassin:

> some of the things here ... will seem at first sight not to be useful ... when everything has been read, it will be clear that they have been put here for a good and rightful purpose.
>
> (Thomassin, M. (*c*.1456) *Registre delphinal*, fol iii verso)

REFERENCES

Backhouse, J. (ed.) (1990) *The Bedford Hours*, London, British Library.

Thomassin, M. (*c*.1456) *Registre delphinal*, Grenoble, Bibliothèque municipale, MS U909.

Kathleen Daly

INTRODUCTION

And gentlemen in England now abed
Shall think themselves accurs'd they were not here,
And hold their manhoods cheap, whiles any speaks
That fought with us upon Saint Crispin's day.
(Shakespeare, 1968, *Henry V*, Act IV, Scene iii)

The king hath granted every article:
His daughter first and then, in sequel, all ...
Only he hath not yet subscribèd this:

Where your majesty demands that the King of France, having any
occasion to write for matter of grant, shall name your highness in this
form, and with this addition, in French, *Notre très cher fils Henri, Roi
d'Angleterre, Héritier de France* [our very dear son, Henry, king of
England, heir of France] ...
(Shakespeare, 1968, *Henry V*, Act V, Scene ii)

Studying an unfamiliar period can be rather like starting in the middle of a
book or watching a single episode of a long-running TV series – the characters
are unfamiliar and you don't know the plot. However, you may well know the
first quotation above from Shakespeare's dramatisation of the battle of
Agincourt (25 October 1415), when Henry V and his army won a resounding
victory against the French. Unless you know the play very well, though, you
may be hard put to identify the second quotation, which is the nearest
Shakespeare, writing at the end of the sixteenth/beginning of the seventeenth
century, gets to telling us about a key historical document, the Treaty of Troyes
(May 1420). As Shakespeare suggests here, the treaty made Henry V heir to
the French kingdom and ruler in all but name.

Of course, in most cases, battles make better drama (and poetry) than treaties.
Agincourt was greeted with great celebrations in England at the time as a God-
given victory and, in both France and England, as divine punishment for the
sins of the French. Nevertheless, it was the Treaty of Troyes, not the battle of
Agincourt, that brought the government of the kingdom of France within
Henry V's grasp, because it was a legal document agreed by the king of France
himself and by the chief representatives of the kingdom. Henry V's son Henry
VI, the only king of England to reign as king of France, owed his title to the
treaty. It was the Treaty of Troyes, again, that set aside the claims of Charles

Figure 1.1   Map of France in the fifteenth century, based on C.T. Allmand (ed.) (1998) *The New Cambridge Medieval History*, vol. 7, *c.1415–c.1500*, Cambridge, Cambridge University Press, Map 8, pp. 393

VI's own surviving son and heir, the dauphin[1] Charles (see the genealogies – Figure I.1 – in the Block Introduction), disrupting the normal line of succession to the throne. Like Agincourt, Charles VII's refusal to accept the treaty and his long struggle to gain the throne of France is the stuff of high drama, thanks to Joan of Arc. This teenage girl emerged from obscurity on the eastern frontiers of France in 1428 to lead French armies to victory against the English at Orleans, and Charles VII to his official coronation at Rheims in 1429. Joan's victory was only a stage in Charles VII's expulsion of the English from France.[2]

As we can see, then, such dramatic events and eye-catching personalities make this a fascinating period, but they can be misleading. We shall be trying to view historical events in context, using a selection of contemporary written sources and pictures.

We shall also be asking questions that link the unit to the course themes:

1   Why was an English king recognised as king of France (beliefs and ideologies)?

 NORMANDY

2   How did the victory of Charles VII over Henry VI affect the development of the French state (the formation of the state)?

I hope that the chronology in the *Course Guide*, the genealogies in the Block Introduction (Figure I.1), the map (Figure 1.1), the list of Valois kings and some English claimants (Table 1.1), and notes in the Anthology will help you navigate through what may be very unfamiliar territory, and that by the end of the unit they will have served their purpose of introducing you to late medieval France and some of the fascinating problems that confront historians of the period.

Table 1.1   Valois kings of France and some English claimants

Valois kings of France	English claimants mentioned in this unit
Philip VI (1327–50)	Edward III (1327–77)
John II (1350–64)	
Charles V (1364–80)	
Charles VI (1380–1422)	Henry V (regent from 1420)
Charles VII (lieutenant-general 1420–22, king 1422–61)	Henry VI (1422–61)
Louis XI (1461–83)	
Charles VIII (1483–98)	
Louis XII (1498–1515)	

---

[1] By the fifteenth century, 'dauphin' (literally, 'dolphin') was the title taken by the king's eldest son and heir to the throne. 'Dauphin' was originally the title of the ruler of the principality of the Dauphiné (see Figure 1.1), which was independent of the kingdom, but was acquired by the kings of France in 1349.

[2] The English retained Calais, which they had first conquered under Edward III in 1347, until 1558.

FROM AGINCOURT TO TROYES

For this section, you will find it helpful to have the chronology and genealogies beside you for reference (see *Course Guide* and Block Introduction).

Why was an English king recognised as king of France? You have probably already worked out that the Treaty of Troyes will play a major part in answering that question, but we need to put this in context by looking briefly at the events that took place between Agincourt and Troyes.

A divided state?

As you may have gathered, Henry V's claim to the crown was not automatically accepted by the French. Military conquest and strategy played a major role in his success. If you look at the chronology in the *Course Guide*, you will see that Henry V had a series of military victories. After the Agincourt campaign of 1415, he returned to France in 1417 to make a much more systematic conquest of the duchy of Normandy, which he had achieved by 1419.

Henry V now became an important player in an existing conflict within France, and he owed much of his success to the internal divisions in the kingdom, notably the rivalry between Armagnacs and Burgundians (see below).

Armagnacs and Burgundians

From 1397, **King Charles VI** of France had suffered from a severe mental illness. This left a power vacuum at the heart of government in which powerful nobles competed for control. By the time of **Henry V**'s second invasion (1417), they had polarised into two main factions: the Burgundians and Armagnacs. The Burgundians were led by the king's cousin, **John the Fearless, duke of Burgundy**. John's lands included not only the duchy of Burgundy and the county of Flanders (see Figure 1.1), but lands outside the frontiers of the French kingdom. The Armagnacs were the remnant of a faction which had originally been led by the king's own brother, **Louis, duke of Orleans**, but John had arranged his assassination in 1407. Louis's followers continued hostilities, which exploded into open civil war in 1410. In 1415, after the disaster of Agincourt, when many leaders of this faction were killed or captured, leadership was taken on by the constable (head) of the royal army, **Bernard, count of Armagnac**, and the faction became known as 'Armagnacs'. In 1418, after 5 years of Armagnac rule, Burgundian supporters in Paris opened the gates to a Burgundian force, and John returned to power. In a series of massacres, the constable of Armagnac and many others were killed. Surviving Armagnacs smuggled the **dauphin** (the future **Charles VII**) out of Paris and a rival government under Charles, who claimed the title of lieutenant-general, was set up south of the Loire, based in Poitiers and Bourges, the apanage that he had inherited from his uncle, **John, duke of Berry** (see Figure 1.2).

Figure 1.2   Princely opulence: John, duke of Berry feasting, *c* 1416, illuminated manuscript painting from the *Très Riches Heures du Duc de Berri,* Musée Condé, Chantilly, France. Photo: Giraudon/Bridgeman Art Library

We shall now look at a primary source. You will find it helpful to look at the advice on working on primary sources in the *Course Guide*. Now read Anthology Document 1.1, from the *Journal of the Citizen of Paris*, bearing in mind what you have read so far in this unit. Make notes on the following questions.

1   Who wrote the document?

2   Who was the intended audience?

3   When was it written?

4   What type of document is it (public, private, official, etc.)?

5   What is its immediate historical context?

6   What can you deduce about the author's attitudes?

Don't worry if you cannot give a clear answer. At this stage it is important to practise analysing a document.

Spend about 20 minutes on this exercise.

1   An anonymous author, possibly a cleric.

2   We do not know.

3   Probably during the Armagnac–Burgundian dispute in 1418–19. We cannot be sure, but the author was in Paris in 1418–19; he may have written this passage at the time or shortly after.

4   This is not an 'official' document; it was written by a private individual.

5   The massacre in Paris of the Armagnacs in 1418 and its aftermath.

6   The author blames the Armagnacs for all France's problems, including defeat at the battle of Agincourt (1415) and the loss of Normandy: even the English are better. The author laments the fate of the king and queen of France, and blames the dauphin for their plight. The source also reflects the author's Christian beliefs.

What is the significance of this document for our study of the period? It gives us some information about the bitterness felt by Parisian citizens towards the Armagnacs and the impact of the departure of Charles the dauphin from Paris.

The citizen of Paris implies that the Armagnacs and Burgundians continued their civil war without paying any attention to the English. In fact, both sides did attempt to make peace, and a meeting was even arranged at Montereau in September 1419 between John and the dauphin. However, motivated by the desire for revenge, because of the Burgundian massacre of the Armagnacs in Paris, some of the dauphin's followers killed John the Fearless. John's heir, Philip the Good, decided to make a separate peace with the English the same year and this became the basis of the Treaty of Troyes.

The Treaty of Troyes

Now turn to Anthology Document 1.2. The Treaty of Troyes (May 1420) between Charles VI and Henry V formed the basis for an English king to succeed to the French throne. As it is quite complex, I have summarised the main points, and their significance, below. I suggest that, as you read my analysis, you look at the numbered clauses in the treaty to see what the original document says.

- Charles VI declares Henry V to be his heir (clause 6). Henry will only rule France after Charles VI's death: until then he is given the title of regent. Henry had inherited an earlier claim to the throne from the English king Edward III (see the genealogies – Figure I.1 – in the Block Introduction), whose mother was directly descended from the last Capetian king, Philip IV. But there is no reference to this in the treaty. By leaving Charles VI as ruler of France, Henry seemed to acknowledge that Charles VI and his predecessors were rightfully kings of France. The treaty establishes a new basis for Henry's rights (that is, the king of France has chosen him as successor), and should bring peace to the two kingdoms (see the opening paragraph – what is known as the 'preamble' of the document). However, Charles VI had a son still living, the dauphin Charles. The treaty acknowledges his existence, but no peace is to be made with him (clause 29). The dauphin's claim to the throne, and his refusal to acknowledge the treaty, was a serious impediment to peace. He had already set up a rival government south of the Loire, and he and his partisans refused to acknowledge the treaty. In January 1421, the dauphin Charles was formally banished for his complicity in the murder of John the Fearless and declared incapable of inheriting the throne, after being tried in his absence at a special session of the Parlement of Paris[3] the previous December. The treaty recognises that the dauphin and his 'Armagnac' followers have to be defeated to bring peace (clause 12).
- All the inhabitants of the kingdom are to swear an oath of allegiance to obey Henry, first as regent during Charles VI's lifetime then as king (clause 13).
- The treaty reflects the duke of Burgundy's importance. He is the only French prince specifically mentioned (clause 27), and the interests of his followers are protected in clauses 15 and 19. So the treaty was an outcome of the internal divisions within France rather than just a consequence of the English invasion. In fact, in the sixteenth century, a Carthusian monk was reputed to have told King Francis I of France that the king of England had entered France through John the Fearless's head: a reference to John's assassination. A breakdown in Anglo-Burgundian relations could undermine the treaty.
- The treaty sets out the basis for the relationship between the two kingdoms of England and France. These should be united after Charles VI's death (clause 24). Each kingdom is to keep its own customs and laws, and they are to be equal in status. It also aims to safeguard the lawful customs of the French kingdom – by implication, Henry V was not to treat the kingdom as

---

[3] The Parlement of Paris was the supreme law court for the French kingdom in the early fifteenth century. It was therefore a legal, not a representative, body. In contrast, the English parliament was more representative (see Unit 3).

if he was a conqueror, as he had been in Normandy. Clauses 14 and 15 provide for the restoration of those who have lost their lands if they swear obedience to Henry V. He will not impose unnecessary or uncustomary taxation (clause 23). The treaty insists that Charles VI's servants shall be French born and French speaking (clause 27).

PART 1

- Normandy is to be reunited with the French crown after Charles VI's death. Interestingly, there is no reference to Guyenne,[4] which English kings claimed by hereditary right, nor Calais, which the English had held since 1347, when it was captured by Edward III.

EXERCISE

Look back quickly over the unit so far and jot down some ideas in answer to the following question:

Why was a king of England recognised as king of France?

Spend about 15 minutes on this exercise.

SPECIMEN ANSWER

By the Treaty of Troyes, the French king, Charles VI, formally recognised Henry V as his heir. The treaty was therefore more important than the claims Henry had inherited from Edward III. Henry's own military victories were also very important, particularly the conquest of Normandy, which allowed him to threaten Paris. However, the context for this success, and for the Treaty of Troyes, was the French king's illness and the civil war between Armagnacs and Burgundians, which culminated in the assassination of John the Fearless (1419) and an alliance between his son Philip the Good and Henry V.

Of course we can use such an important source to pose other questions. For example, when you revise this unit you may want to analyse it as a source of information about the French state at the time, using the criteria in the Block Introduction.

FROM THE TREATY OF TROYES (1420) TO THE EXPULSION OF THE ENGLISH (1449–53)

Henry V's death on 31 August 1422, a few months before that of Charles VI on 21 October, meant that the English king never succeeded to the French throne. His son by Catherine of France succeeded at the age of nine months as Henry VI, and Henry V's brother John, duke of Bedford, became regent. This established what has been described as the Dual Monarchy (the union of the two crowns) or the Anglo-Burgundian regime (highlighting its dependence on the support of the duke of Burgundy), or 'the English occupation' (by some French historians). Royal minorities were rarely good news for medieval kingdoms, and the situation was compounded by the fact that Henry VI's father, Henry V, failed to defeat Charles the dauphin or to gain general acceptance of the Treaty of Troyes south of the Loire. The dauphin claimed the

---

[4] Also spelled Guienne and sometimes referred to as Aquitaine.

Figure 1.3   Charles VII: portrait by Jean Fouquet, mid fifteenth century, oil on wood, 86 x 71 cm, Louvre, Paris. Photo: © RMN / © Hervé Lewandowski

title of king of France (as Charles VII – see Figure 1.3) on his father's death. In 1429, he was finally consecrated king in Rheims cathedral.

There was a long minority in England and rivalry in the royal council. Henry VI remained in England and was not formally crowned king of France until 1431, which seemed to have been a rushed response to his rival's recent coronation. The Dual Monarchy retained Paris until 1436, when the city fell to Charles VII's troops. Though Henry VI continued to claim the French crown, his power was then limited to Normandy, where the English administration established itself until Charles VII conquered the duchy in 1449. Between 1451 and 1453, the English king even lost the duchy of Guyenne, and the only land he and his successors held in France was Calais. English rule in France effectively ended in 1453.

Now read Anne Curry, *The Hundred Years War*, in the secondary sources on the course website. This is an extract from a textbook covering the conflict. Curry is writing the book within a particular series, 'British History in Perspective', which explains her concentration on factors affecting the English. However, it is a clear, short account of the main events.

Note down the reasons Curry gives in this extract for the collapse of English power in France up to 1451.

You should take no more than 30 minutes to complete this exercise.

The Treaty of Troyes failed to bring peace. Curry identifies the years 1420–44 as the 'longest continuous period of open warfare' in the Hundred Years War. The English failed even to secure the area around Paris; failed to breach the Loire in 1429 (when their siege of the city of Orleans was lifted); lost Paris in 1436. By the mid 1430s, even Normandy was threatened by revolt, and the English never really recovered full control of the duchy. Curry also emphasises the reliance of the English regime in France on English troops and money (in spite of the expectation after the Treaty of Troyes that France itself would pay these costs).

The Treaty of Arras between France and Burgundy (1435) removed the most important ally of the English in France. Philip's renunciation of the Treaty of Troyes at Arras in 1435 was devastating to the English cause.

A bungled attempt by the English to pressurise another ally, the duke of Brittany, into a closer alliance by the seizure of Fougères gave Charles VII an excuse to renew the war in 1449: Normandy fell in 1449–50, Guyenne followed in 1451. 'As in 1420, military success was the eventual arbiter of who should be king of France'.

The Anglo-Burgundian alliance was crucial to the success of the Treaty of Troyes. Philip's withdrawal from the Anglo-Burgundian alliance opened the way for the fall of Paris, the French capital and seat of government. Guy Thompson's study of the city under the Dual Monarchy demonstrates that the city was basically a Burgundian regime with an English veneer. By 1436, the English were unable to send sufficient support and troops to defend the city (Thompson, 1991, pp. 26–45). In contrast, part of Guyenne (led by the town of Bordeaux) revolted against Charles VII in 1452, with the aid of an English army, and had to be reconquered in 1453. Calais remained in English hands, and continued to be used as a base for expeditions against France, until it was finally lost in 1558.

THE EXPERIENCE OF OCCUPATION

We shall now turn to the theme of beliefs and ideologies. What did it mean to French men and women to be ruled by a foreign king?

Even before the siege of Orleans, only France north of the Loire acknowledged Henry VI as king, and only the area around Paris and the duchy of Normandy were effectively under his control for any length of time. Guyenne had a much longer history of attachment to the English (stretching back to the twelfth century), although the area under English control had fluctuated in the course of the Hundred Years War. Malcolm Vale has even challenged the notion that the English in Guyenne could be regarded as an 'enemy' occupation (Vale, 1998, p. 402).

We shall therefore be concentrating on French reactions in Paris and Normandy.

Asking what it meant to such French men and women to be governed by an English king is an interesting question in its own right, but it is part of a wider debate. Were the English defeated because the French refused to accept a foreign ruler? History has a tendency to be written by the victors, and there is a long strand of historical writing – beginning with Charles VII's contemporaries – that presented the defeat of the English as 'inevitable'. Nineteenth-century, and some twentieth-century, historians have seized on examples of resistance to English occupation as evidence of patriotism for France and a French king that spelled doom for Henry VI's regime.

However, this approach ignores Henry VI's claim to be the legitimate ruler of France under the terms of the Treaty of Troyes. What methods were used by Henry VI's government to persuade French subjects that Henry was the rightful king of France?

There were certainly attempts to convince Henry's French subjects of his legitimacy. From November 1422, the union of the crowns of France and England, symbolised by their two coats of arms side by side, appeared on a whole series of new French silver and gold coins. In one case (a gold coin known as a *salute*, minted in 1423), the figure of the Virgin Mary appears behind a shield with the arms of France, and the angel, announcing the birth of her son, Jesus Christ (Gospel According to St Luke, 1.26–38), behind that of England. J.W. McKenna suggested that contemporaries would have made a link between the annunciation of the birth of Christ the Saviour to Mary (and thus religious salvation) and the birth of Henry VI, who was to 'save' France from warfare and bring peace (McKenna, 1965, p. 147).

EXERCISE

Now turn to Anthology Document 1.3, an account of the processions and festivities that greeted Henry VI's entry into Paris for his coronation in 1431. Accounts such as this are particularly valuable because they are our only record of a fleeting event. If you are still unsure about analysing documents, the *Course Guide* will help you identify important features. However, I shall not be spelling them all out here. Instead, we are going to use the document just to answer the following question:

What can we learn from this document about Parisian attitudes to Henry VI as king of France in 1431?

Spend about 30 minutes on this exercise.

SPECIMEN ANSWER

The source implies that no expense was spared in setting up the entry ceremonies. The major dignitaries of Paris are very evident, greeting the king on behalf of the city. The procession passes many of the major landmarks in the city, which symbolise civic as well as royal power. There are clearly some 'tableaux' (mimes), rather like gild or mystery plays (such as the well-known Coventry mystery cycle in medieval England), which emphasise the loyalty of the French people (and particularly the city) to the king. Others seem to be purely for entertainment (such as the pursuit of the stag).

Well done if you picked out the symbol of the Dual Monarchy – the two shields, and the elaborate combination of images and verses at the Châtelet.

Let us now take two examples of ways historians have interpreted this primary source. On the one hand, McKenna concluded that:

> The symbolism contrived on this occasion for the welcome of Henry VI to Paris marked the zenith of English political propaganda in France, a monument to Bedford's efforts to win over French sympathies.
>
> (McKenna, 1965, p. 160)

On the other hand, Thompson looked at another set of source materials: the accounts of the city government of Paris. He was able to show that most of the organisation of – and, more importantly, payment for – the celebrations came not from the royal entourage, but from the city's ruling council and the Parisians (Thompson, 1991, pp. 198–205).

> Their concern was to bring the city of Paris to the minds of the royal party and stress the king's obligations to its people … the emphasis is on Paris, and on the duties owed by the king in return for the loyalty symbolised in the pageantry. [Usually] the king's Frenchness is emphasised. 'Fleurs de lys' adorned the canopy above his head and 'fleurs de lys [of the shield of France]' featured at the Porte St-Denis … No dual-monarchy symbolism was to be seen except in the tableau at the Châtelet. A presentation of scenes from the life of St Denis [a patron saint of the monarchy] was essentially French, and the accompanying poem reminded the king of his duty to defend the faith as his predecessors had done.
>
> (Thompson, 1991, p. 203)

The only item not represented in the accounts studied by Thompson was the tableau at the Châtelet, and he concluded that it might indeed have been organised and paid for by the royal council. The council included Anglo-Burgundian supporters, who understood how to use traditional French symbolism to support a king of France who happened to be half-English. The entry ceremony was already well established in France, and its semi-religious symbolism had evolved over the course of the preceding century. By the fifteenth century, the entry was essentially 'a dialogue between a more approachable king and his less passive subjects'; in the case of Paris, Thompson concluded it was more in the nature of a civic monologue!

By looking at a wider range of sources than McKenna, Thompson is able to reinterpret the entry of Henry VI into Paris as more than 'English' propaganda, and gives a more nuanced picture of relations between the French and English in Paris. But was this situation typical or exceptional? Thompson has found other examples of Burgundian supporters who continued to serve under the Dual Monarchy: for example, Pierre Cauchon, bishop of Beauvais (who was one of Joan of Arc's judges at her trial). Some Frenchmen were so committed to the English, or implicated in the regime, that they fled from Charles VII's advance, leaving Paris for Normandy (after 1436), then for England (after 1449). There is also evidence of intermarriage between English and French lower down the social scale. It seems that many French families in 'English' France hedged their bets to preserve their offices and property, some staying in Paris to serve under Henry VI, others leaving to serve Charles (VII) as dauphin, then king. Such evidence shows that, as historians, we have to be careful of generalising about 'French' reactions to an 'English' occupation.

Normandy – resistance or compliance?

Can we find similar ambivalence in Norman attitudes to the English?

The duchy of Normandy was one of the richest provinces of France. It gave the English vital control over the Channel, so they could provision their armies. They could also keep open the route from England to Paris, the capital of France and the seat of royal government. These facts explain why Henry V chose to start his conquest in Normandy, rather than in Guyenne or Calais (see Figure 1.1).

Henry V claimed to be the legitimate duke of Normandy (the French king had confiscated it from an English king in 1204). A combination of carrot and stick were used to impose and maintain English rule. Those who swore an oath of allegiance to Henry V kept their possessions, those who refused were treated as rebels – their lands were confiscated and redistributed to Englishmen. Some of the greatest noble landowners, such as the duke of Alençon, joined Charles VII. Most of the lesser nobility stayed, although they seemed equally willing to change sides when Charles VII reconquered the duchy. However, clergy and towns accepted English rule. On the other hand, there is evidence of a succession of plots to deliver Norman towns to the partisans of Charles VII and of an extensive rebellion in the Caux region in 1436. To what extent is this evidence of 'national sentiment' and hostility to English 'occupation'? What other factors need to be taken into account?

We shall start by looking at two different types of evidence of reactions to life in 'English' Normandy. This will also give you further skills in using primary sources, as it gives you the chance to compare two different types of document.

EXERCISE

First look at the extract from Thomas Basin's *History of Charles VII* (Anthology Document 1.4b). (You might also find it helpful to look at Anthology Document 1.4a, Basin's description of his early years.) Now compare Anthology Document 1.4b with the letter of remission for Jean Maunourry (Anthology Document 1.5), and read the head notes carefully.

What conclusions do you draw about sentiments towards the English in the duchy?

[handwritten margin notes:] See "Read" Chapter 17 p 396

Spend about 30 minutes on this exercise.

We could use these sources to argue that *some* French were hostile to the English and regarded them as invaders. Basin's story of the priest suggests that brigandage was linked to patriotism: once the English left, it would cease (Basin, with the benefit of hindsight, says that this was the case). Jean Maunourry cries out in a tavern words in support of 'the crown of France' and the duke of Alençon (a leading Norman nobleman who had joined Charles VII). Nevertheless, both sources hint at the complexity of relations between the English and the Normans. Did Maunourry really sell a horse to the Armagnacs because he supported Charles VII, or for purely economic reasons? Or was he 'framed' by his enemies, as the letter of remission alleged? Basin's 'brigands' may hate the English but they are also desperate or fugitives from justice.

Patriots or brigands? The debate over Norman loyalties

The historical debate about the brigands is closely linked to debates over whether 'national sentiment' existed in France in the fifteenth century.

The French historian Lefèvre-Pontalis, writing in the late nineteenth/early twentieth centuries, saw brigands as patriots, while English historians distinguished between 'political' opponents, and what we might almost term 'economic refugees', who resorted to robbery when they lost their livelihood through economic crisis (which preceded the English occupation) or the effects of war.

Historians have also detected change over time in Normandy. War in 1417–19 and crushing taxes in 1420–22 led people to desert their lands. Between the battle of Verneuil and the relief of Orleans, Normandy was relatively secure from Charles VII's troops, and the economy revived. Then Normandy was once again in the front line and paid heavy taxation, while Charles's successes may have encouraged some Normans to support him. The effects of war, famine and epidemics promoted 'economic' brigandage. English soldiers turned brigand when they were not paid their wages. If you have time and you want to find out more about this debate, we have included an extract from Allmand's discussion in the secondary sources (Allmand, *Lancastrian Normandy: The History of a Medieval Occupation 1415–50*). This debate shows how difficult it is to distinguish patriotic or national sentiment from issues of crime, law and order (of course this is not just a medieval phenomenon, as you will see when you look at Block 5, Unit 17).

What is clear is the severe economic, social and political crisis to which Normandy was subject in the 1430s and early 1440s. In October 1435, in the wake of the treaty of Arras, Dieppe fell to the French in a surprise attack. This sparked off an uprising among the peasants of the Caux region (eastern Normandy), who marched through Normandy and threatened the duchy's capital, Rouen. Although they enlisted a few of Charles VII's French captains as their leaders, the rising seems to have been spontaneous.

Thomas Basin is a major source for the background to the rising and the rising itself. He describes how the peasants acted in self-defence against the brigands, and how they turned against the English in the insurrection. However, poorly armed, they were cut to pieces by English forces. Basin also alleged that the peasants were betrayed by Charles VII's French captains (Bois, 1984, p. 338).

The rising was ferociously suppressed by the English. Bois noted that some villages in the region seem to have been entirely deserted, paying no tithes. Bad harvests led to famine in 1436–39; shortages led English garrisons in Norman towns to live off the countryside, making the situation worse.

The economic crisis in Normandy was particularly grave because of the reliance of the English regime on income from the duchy, particularly in the form of taxation. Even before the fall of Paris, Normandy paid far and away the lion's share. As the French became more of a threat, demands for money rose. Allmand has calculated that, between 1434 and 1440, an annual average of 344,000 livres tournois was voted by the Norman estates. But the representatives in these assemblies, normally about sixty, were drawn from a very narrow group who were loyal to the English regime. Neither the clergy nor the nobility paid tax, and the third estate was represented by the urban middle class, whereas most of the tax burden fell on the countryside. The Caux region was the 'granary of eastern Normandy' but could not pay its way after the rising, leaving a much heavier burden on the remainder of the duchy (the administrative districts of Caen and the Cotentin). By 1439, there was increasing resistance in the estates to voting large sums, there were delays in collecting it (one instalment of a tax voted in 1443 was not collected in full before 1449) and widespread tax evasion. Although the truce of Tours of 1444 brought the end of open warfare, while the search for a permanent peace continued, taxes still had to be levied to pay the Norman garrisons (Allmand, 1983, pp. 176–83).

CHARLES VII AND 'NATIONAL SENTIMENT'

So far we have concentrated on the issue of national sentiment within territory claimed by Henry VI. It is now time to look at the role of Charles VII's supporters. Even before the Treaty of Troyes, an anonymous partisan of the dauphin warned 'loyal Frenchmen' against attempts by the Burgundians and English to make peace. This was couched as an 'appeal' to loyal subjects to fight for the fleurs de lis – as we have seen, this heraldic emblem was used to symbolise France. The author also warned French subjects not to trust the English, alleging that the English used Latin in their treaties to mislead the French!

Joan of Arc

Things had arrived at such a point that there seemed no hope that the lord king [Charles VII] could deliver his lands by human aid, as the power of his enemies and those disobedient to him was continually growing ... It was then that it pleased the Almighty to send a ... young maid.

(Gélu [1429], cited in Contamine, 1992a, p. 100)

The quotation above is from a memoir by Jacques Gélu, archbishop of Embrun, addressed to Charles VII in May 1429. This contemporary view sums up a current of historical interpretation which lasted into the twentieth century: that Charles VII, and France, were saved by Joan of Arc, who wakened a sense of national identity (see Figure 1.4). It is difficult to see Joan purely in a medieval context because she has been invoked as a symbol of French patriotism and resistance to invaders over succeeding centuries (she was a favourite of General de Gaulle, leader of the Free French during the Second World War). Joan's canonisation (official recognition as a saint) in 1920 also reflects a complex historical situation. It was promoted by groups in France who wished to see the restoration of the monarchy and who were fearful of the

Figure 1.4   Joan of Arc besieging Paris: a late-fifteenth-century miniature accompanying a poem commemorating the deeds of Charles VII, Bibliothèque nationale de France, Paris, FR 5054, f. 66v. Photo: The Bridgeman Art Library, London

impact of secularism and atheism, concerns shared by the papacy (Warner, 1991, pp. 261–5).

Joan, the daughter of tenant farmers, was born in 1412 on the eastern frontiers of France. She was convinced that she had a divine mission to secure Charles VII's coronation as king and to drive the English out of France. She persuaded the king and his advisers to let her lead an army to relieve Orleans. Joan wrote to Henry VI and to Philip of Burgundy, ordering them to withdraw their troops, without success. On 29 April 1429 she reached Orleans with an army and relieved the town, entering it on 8 May, and on 17 July she escorted Charles VII to his coronation at Rheims, which his supporters had taken from English and Burgundian troops. Joan's success was short-lived: she fell into Burgundian hands, was sold to the English, tried as a heretic (because she was accused of falsely claiming divine inspiration) and burnt at Rouen on 30 May 1431 (Vale, 1974, pp. 45–6). Joan's family was far more concerned to clear her than was Charles VII. They lobbied the pope, and in 1456 a panel of clerics led by Jean Juvénal des Ursins, archbishop of Rheims, annulled her sentence for heresy.

EXERCISE

Read Anthology Document 1.6, 'Letter from Joan of Arc to the duke of Burgundy'. What can you learn from it about Joan's beliefs about the king and kingdom of France?

Spend about 10 minutes on this exercise.

SPECIMEN ANSWER

Joan asserts the holiness of the kingdom of France and its direct protection by God. She declares that by fighting against the 'loyal French', the duke will be fighting against Jesus Christ himself.

There is little doubt about Joan's own sincerity. Did she have a key role in defeating the English? This view was expressed by some contemporaries, and followed by French historians such as Joseph Calmette and Eugène Déprez (Contamine, 1992b).

It is hard to disentangle Joan's role from the general fear of an English onslaught across the Loire, which was instrumental in allowing Charles to reimpose taxation (see below), or the impact of his coronation at Rheims, which enhanced his claim to be the rightful king of France.

Joan does seem to have had a key role in galvanising Charles's troops at the siege of Orleans. Her victories certainly undermined English morale. However, her influence lasted only as long as she kept defeating the English. Charles's victories after Joan's death were probably more influential in winning him support (the capture of Paris in 1436, the conquest of Normandy and Guyenne from 1449 to 1453). He did not need an intermediary such as Joan to show that he had divine approval for his kingship. For example, he claimed that his conquest of Normandy was miraculous, and instituted a religious holiday to celebrate his victory (see Anthology Document 1.7).

To sum up, it is difficult to quantify the extent of support for Charles VII and hostility to the English because of the patchy nature of the evidence and the difficulties of interpreting it. It is easier to detect material reasons for the English defeat, such as the withdrawal of Burgundian support, the failure of the Treaty of Troyes to bring peace, and the economic and social crisis in Normandy, made worse by continual demands for tax to pay for defence against Charles VII's supporters. To that we must add the relative strength of Charles VII's resources by 1449. He was also willing to win over support from nobles, churchmen and office holders, rather than punish those who had submitted to the English.

THE FRENCH STATE

How did the struggle of Charles VII and Henry VI affect the development of the French state?

Drawing on ideas about the state in the Block Introduction, we shall consider:

- territory and sovereignty
- a sense of common identity among the French
- the powers of the crown
- the growth of an administration in state service.

Territory

The relationship between the king and his kingdom can be difficult to grasp because it was essentially a two-tier system. The king had extensive theoretical claims over large parts of France, but only exercised real authority in areas that he ruled directly, known as the royal domain. Between the thirteenth and the fifteenth centuries, by conquest, purchase and inheritance, kings of France gradually extended their domain from a small kernel of lands around Paris to most territories in France. This domain, however, was constantly fluctuating. The king had obligations to provide for the royal family in the form of apanages, grants of rights and lands made to his sons from his domain. Direct control then passed to his relatives. If the direct male line of succession failed, these lands reverted to the crown, but were often granted out again.

The recovery of Normandy, in particular, brought major financial gains to Charles VII, but he also made substantial grants of lands to his supporters. The capture of the duchy of Guyenne was prestigious for the crown, because English claims to the duchy went back to the twelfth century. However, Louis XI granted first Normandy then Guyenne to his brother Charles (though Louis recovered Normandy as soon as he could and recovered Guyenne when Charles died without heirs).

By expelling the English from France (except Calais), however, Charles was able to reunite a kingdom formerly divided along the Loire.

Sovereignty: beliefs and ideologies

> To the king pertains sovereignty and supreme jurisdiction in all the kingdom ... this sovereignty and final jurisdiction are by such manner conjoined and annexed to the Crown that they cannot be separated from it because they are the principal nobilities (dignities) of the Crown.
>
> *(Songe du Verger* [1378], cited by O'Meara, 2001, p. 122)[5]

> The king of France has God alone as his sovereign in earthly matters, and recognises no other and has full rights of absolute sovereignty in all his kingdom.
>
> *(Mirouer historial abregié de France*, 1451, f. 219)[6]

The first quotation comes from the *Songe du Verger*, one of the most important texts for understanding political thinking about the French crown at the end of the fourteenth century. The author was probably Évrart de Trémaugon, a Breton who became bishop of Dol and counsellor of King Charles V of France (ruled 1365–80), at a date when the king had recovered most of the gains made in France by Edward III. The second quotation comes from a list of the powers of the king of France in a much less well-known work, probably by a royal counsellor Noël de Fribois.

They show a remarkable similarity, partly because the *Songe* was a very influential text. But the very fact that the same ideas were cited at a distance of sixty years or so also reflects continuity in thinking about the powers of the crown, at least by royal servants. Recent events nevertheless seem to contradict the authors' assertions. In the fourteenth century, Philip VI and John II had been defeated by the English and John II had actually been captured and ransomed. In the fifteenth century France was divided by civil wars and English invasion.

Both texts claim that the French crown has supreme authority in the French kingdom, rather than only in various territories that kings governed directly (through conquest, marriage and inheritance). One of the key developments of the medieval and early modern period was the way in which such theoretical claims came to coincide with the realities of royal government.

These quotations link the exercise of supreme power (sovereignty) closely with the exercise of justice. The king's role as the guardian and administrator of justice was a key factor in the extension of his power and authority throughout the kingdom. The king had to exercise much of his power through intermediaries, such as his great vassals, who technically owed him loyalty because they held their lands by his permission, but whose power often made

---

[5] *Le Songe du Verger* (The Dream in the Orchard), vol. 2, p. 202, translated and cited by O'Meara (2001), p. 122. The *Songe* was a translation and reworking of a Latin version, *The Somnium viridarii* (1376), also composed for Charles V.

[6] Abridged Historical Mirror of France.

them almost independent of royal control. However, their subjects could appeal over their heads to royal courts, and particularly the supreme court of appeal, the Parlement of Paris. These quotations also emphasise that the king's only superior is God. We are now going to explore the way a visual source can help us understand these aspects of royal government.

Looking at visual sources: the royal image

In the *Course Guide*, you read some advice on how to look at pictures. When we looked at the Clovis miniature (in the Block Introduction), you saw that we need a lot of background information to understand medieval images. Now look at *Visual Sources*, Plate 1.1, and Figures 1.5–1.8.

Figure 1.5 will help you identify the people in the painting. I am now going to give you a description of the painting, together with some information about its context, before you answer a question about it.

Figure 1.5 *The Crucifixion of the Parlement of Paris*: silhouette of painting

Description

Figure 1.6 shows the left-hand side of the painting. *St Louis* (1226–1270), crowned, carries a sceptre in his right hand. He is wearing a blue mantle decorated with stylised lilies – the heraldic emblem also found on the French royal coat of arms. St Louis's piety and justice made him a model for his successors. He was canonised by the pope in 1297, after extensive lobbying by Louis's grandson Philip IV. St Louis's face may be based on an official portrait of Charles VII, but we have no independent evidence for this.

St John the Baptist wears a red cloak and a hairy garment. According to the New Testament (Gospel of St Matthew, 3), John the Baptist preached the coming of Christ in 'a raiment of camel's hair'. In medieval paintings, John was often shown with a lamb, which was a symbol for the 'lamb of God', that is, Christ. St Louis seems to be pointing to John, and may be indicating a close connection with him. John was venerated by the kings of France: his relics were kept near the Parlement of Paris, in the Ste-Chapelle (Holy chapel) built for St Louis. How paintings look today is not necessarily how they appeared originally, since many were damaged and repaired over time. In this case, John's face has been repainted, probably in the nineteenth century (Lorentz and Comblen-Sonkes, 2001, pp. 114–20).

Behind the saints are views of Paris, and in the background are three figures looking at the river Seine. One holds a scroll in his hand, looking like a plaintiff from the parlement. The building to the left of St Louis is the Tour de Nesle, and across the river we can see the Louvre, the ancient fortress and palace of the French kings (now the site of the modern Louvre art gallery and museum) (Lorentz and Comblen-Sonkes, 2001, pp. 114–20).

Figure 1.7 shows the central section of the painting. In the centre is the crucifixion itself, with the Virgin Mary weeping on the left, accompanied by female saints, Christ on the cross, and St John the Evangelist on the right. The inclusion of the Virgin and St John the Evangelist was quite common in crucifixion scenes. Above Christ's head is the figure of God the Father, with a dove descending to Christ (a representation of the Holy Spirit). According to the New Testament, Christ was crucified on Golgotha, the place of the skull (there are bones and a skull at the foot of the cross). The tower and dome in the rear probably represent Jerusalem.

Figure 1.8 shows the right-hand side of the painting. *St Denis* (seen here holding his own severed head) was believed to have converted the French from paganism, and to have been martyred on Montmartre. He had a special significance for French monarchs, whose bodies were buried in his abbey near Paris.

The emperor Charlemagne was king of the Franks before he became emperor of the west in 800 CE. He was regarded as a French monarch, as an ancestor of the ruling king, and also as a saint, though he was never formally canonised by any pope (a condition for 'official' sainthood).

Figure 1.6 *The Crucifixion of the Parlement of Paris*, detail, left panel, mid fifteenth century, oil on wood, 2.26 x 2.7 m. Louvre, Paris. Photo © RMN / © Jean-Gilles Berizzi

Figure 1.7   *The Crucifixion of the Parlement of Paris*, detail, centre panel, mid fifteenth century, oil on wood, 2.26 x 2.7 m. Louvre, Paris. Photo © RMN / © Jean-Gilles Berizzi

Figure 1.8 *The Crucifixion of the Parlement of Paris*, detail, right panel, mid fifteenth century, oil on wood, 2.26 x 2.7 m. Louvre, Paris. Photo © RMN / © Jean-Gilles Berizzi

Context: the Parlement of Paris

Before Charles VII's reign, the Parlement of Paris had been the supreme royal law court. The court had been affected by the Armagnac–Burgundian dispute, as there were purges of its members when the rival parties gained power, although only 11 per cent actually lost office as a result (Autrand, 1969, pp. 322, 324). After 1418, the Parlement of Poitiers (under Charles as dauphin, then king) and the Parlement of Paris (under the Dual Monarchy) both claimed to be the supreme court. In 1436, after the recovery of Paris, Charles VII reintegrated the personnel of the Parlement of Poitiers with that of Paris, so few lost their offices. The Parlement of Paris was also the forum for some of the most extreme claims for royal power, from advocates and proctors pleading for the king's rights against other parties.

The purpose of the painting

At the end of the Middle Ages, court rooms traditionally had such paintings of the crucifixion of Jesus Christ (known as 'calvaries'). This painting had a didactic, or teaching, purpose. While administering justice on the king's behalf, the magistrates were to follow the example of pious and just kings from the past, and avoid bad examples, symbolised by the crucifixion of Christ and the beheading of St Denis. The painting hung where members of the parlement could see it – in the *grande chambre* (great hall, principal court), where it replaced an old-fashioned painting made in about 1406. The magistrates themselves paid for the new painting and it is reasonable to assume they decided on the subject matter, choosing a new type of style (characterised by the use of perspective, realism and carefully observed detail) that had developed in the Low Countries. Who was the artist who painted this image? Most recently he has been identified with a northern artist (christened the 'Master of Dreux Budé' after another altarpiece he painted for a royal notary and secretary of that name) (Lorentz and Comblen-Sonkes, 2001, pp. 114–20; Thiébaut, Lorentz and Martin, 2004, pp. 92–3).

EXERCISE

What can we learn from this image about the way the monarchy was depicted in fifteenth-century France?

You may find it helpful to consult the section on analysing visual sources in the Tutor-Marked Assignment Booklet.

Spend about 30 minutes on this exercise.

SPECIMEN ANSWER

The presence of the saintly patrons of the French monarchy emphasises divine protection of the ruler and the king's duty as a guardian of justice. The theme of this painting is kingship, rather than an individual king. The ruler 'embodies' his kingdom and people, or, as we might say, the 'state'.

We cannot tell from the painting alone whether this exalted view of the king of France was widely held; we have to remember that it was painted to remind members of the parlement of their duty. We could argue that royal institutions like the Parlement of Paris really give us more information about aspirations, than about the real ability of the crown to impose its power in the French kingdom.

However, we have already seen similar use of symbols in other sources (Henry VI's entry into Paris, the Clovis miniature).

A common identity?

Earlier in the unit, we saw that evidence about national sentiment can be difficult to interpret. So why is it important to historians?

> Kings of France had to exploit ceremonial and propaganda to *invent* ... the country they governed, to give it unity and form, to create loyalty to a[n] ... ideal of France ... As for national identity, this was above all encouraged by emphasising the religious mission of the monarchy ... It is thus hardly surprising that the invention of France – most nations are after all formed by people united by a common error concerning their ancestry and a shared hostility to their neighbours ... – was a slow process, marked by many reverses.
>
> (Jones, 2003, pp. 20–1)

Jones sums up a school of historical thought in which ideas and beliefs about the monarchy are as important in explaining why royal power expanded as more material powers, like taxation (which we will come to later). Some have concluded that a common sense of identity did exist in later medieval France, even though it was very different from modern citizenship. It included a close sense of identification with the monarchy and royal symbols. The fleur de lis was not only the royal coat of arms (as we saw in the Clovis miniature), it was also a symbol for France. France was also depicted as a queen (probably drawing on the image of the Virgin Mary, who was also represented as a queen, and who was believed to have a special affection for France). In the *Quadrilogue invectif*, a dialogue between France and the three estates, composed in 1422 and written in support of Charles VII, Alain Chartier used the image of France as a queen deserted by her subjects, the three estates, who quarrel among themselves instead of fighting the English (see Figure 1.9).

History was another potentially unifying factor. The monarchy's story was linked with that of the French people in the *Grandes Chroniques de France* (Great Chronicles of France), composed in 1274, which by the fifteenth century was the most widely disseminated history of France. It incorporated older traditions, such as the myth that the French people originated from refugees from Troy, and thus had a common origin. However, the text is structured around the reigns of kings of France, so that they become the thread linking the past to the present. Illustrations in manuscripts of this text could also draw attention to themes favourable to the monarchy, and hostile to its enemies (as in Figure 1.10).

As we have seen elsewhere in the unit, supporters of Charles VII and Henry VI drew on the past to justify their claim to rule. After Charles VII's victories, Noël de Fribois, a royal counsellor, used history to show that the English (denounced as barbarians and even cannibals) had no right to govern the

Figure 1.9   The state divided. France, represented as a queen, tries to support the kingdom (a crumbling building) unaided by the three estates (clergy, nobility, commoners). From a late-fifteenth century manuscript of Alain Chartier's *Le Quadrilogue invectif* and *Le Livre de l'Espérance*. Bibliothèque nationale de France, FR 24441, f. 5v. Photo: Bibliothèque nationale de France, Paris

Figure 1.10 A royalist interpretation of the relationship between France and England in the *Grandes Chroniques de France*: Edward I kneels to pay homage to King Philip IV of France in 1286. The French royal coat of arms, azure with gold *fleurs de lis*, on the canopy of the throne and the walls dominates the miniature. The English king is shown wearing the English royal coat of arms (three gold lions on a red ground), as if he is paying homage for England. In fact, he paid homage for his lands in France (Guyenne). From Jean Fouquet's illustration of the *Grandes Chroniques de France* (mid fifteenth century), probably Charles VII's own copy. Bibliothèque nationale de France, Paris, FR 6465, fol. 301v. Photo: AKG, London

French kingdom, and openly admitted that when he came to write about them he could not restrain his pen.[7]

This sense of national identity coexisted with a strong sense of regional identity, but was not necessarily incompatible with it. We have seen references to a patron of the monarchy, St Denis, in Henry VI's entry into Paris, and the *Crucifixion of the Parlement of Paris*. St Denis was a northern saint – his chief abbey was on the outskirts of Paris – so it is not surprising to find him commemorated in an event and a picture produced there. In our period, his cult seems to have remained local. However, other regions contributed their own local cults associated with the monarchy. Charles VII's exile south of the Loire stimulated the cult of Clovis (who was never officially canonised) as a saint, particularly around Poitiers. In the fifteenth century, the cult of St Louis spread from the area around Paris to the northern borders of France and south to the 'kingdom of Bourges'. But it was not 'national': it was not celebrated in the south-west (Guyenne) or Burgundy (Beaune, 1985, pp. 77–187).

This clustering of local traditions around the monarchy was also evident in historical writing. Fribois, of Norman origin, even made William the Conqueror, the Norman duke who defeated the English in 1066, a model for Charles VII. In the Dauphiné, which was not even technically part of France, Mathieu Thomassin linked the history of the province to that of the crown. He claimed the principality had played a crucial role in saving Charles VII from his enemies through the valour of its nobility. The Dauphiné bathed in reflected glory through its association with the 'most Christian king' who ruled 'by the grace of God', His 'vicar in temporal matters ... with no sovereign other than God'. Clearly Thomassin was not alone in his views: the Dauphiné was loyal to Charles VII in 1456, when the dauphin Louis (the future Louis XI) quarrelled with his father and fled to Burgundy, and Charles took direct control of the principality. In contrast, the dukes of Brittany made themselves a focus of local traditions, and encouraged a view of the past that exalted Breton independence against France (Daly, 2000a, pp. 124–44).

The powers of the crown

Taxation and troops

> In this world nothing can be said to be certain, except death and taxes.
>   (Benjamin Franklin, 1789)

> 'Alas poor *aides*, go you to the war!'
>   (Jean Juvénal des Ursins, 1445 (Lewis, 1968, p. 108))

In the fourteenth and fifteenth centuries, the king was expected to live, as far as possible, on the income he derived from his lands and rights (the 'royal domain'); in practice, by the fifteenth century these accounted only for 2–3 per cent of his total income. Alongside this principle, it was accepted that the king

---

[7] Abridged chronicle of France, 1459.

taxes

could levy taxation from his subjects to meet extraordinary needs for the 'public good' (for example, defending his kingdom against invasion).

The development of royal taxation in Charles VII's reign has caused controversy, which has hinged on his fiscal reforms from 1428 to 1445. In *The Fiscal System of Renaissance France*, Martin Wolfe (1972) argued that these changes were so significant that they laid the basis for government without the subjects' consent, and for the development of a royal monopoly of power, known as 'absolutism', which was a characteristic of the 'ancien régime' (the name given to the French monarchy from the late fifteenth century to the French Revolution in 1789). In contrast, David Potter has argued that 'the essential features of a "modern" tax system were in place' by the end of the *fourteenth* century (Potter, 2002, p. 172). The system had evolved to meet the cost of defence during the fourteenth-century phase of the Hundred Years War (from 1337 to 1396), and to pay the ransom of the French king, John the Good, whom the English had captured at the battle of Poitiers in 1356. By the last decades of the fourteenth century, 'taxes had become permanent and more or less essential to the monarchy' (Potter, 2002, p. 174). The chief taxes were the *aides*, an indirect tax on sales and commerce (including a tax on salt, the *gabelle*) and the *taille*, a tax on income. At their inception, these taxes were voted by national representative assemblies (estates general) or regional assemblies or 'estates', comprising the clergy, nobility and third estate (commoners). However, by the end of the fourteenth century, in practice, these taxes were levied without summoning the estates. There was a network of royal tax collectors, but taxation was always a matter of bargaining with local communities. The *taille* was limited in geographical scope, however, as it was not paid in Flanders, Burgundy or Brittany (Potter, 2002. p.176).

VARIANT ①

HISTORICAL DEBATE

VARIANT ②

In the political crisis of 1418 royal power to tax was severely restricted. Indirect taxes were abolished first by John the Fearless, then by the dauphin Charles, south of the Loire. Charles was so weak financially that he had to seek funds from meetings of regional estates in the 1420s. Ironically it was the English threat to Orleans in 1428, an obvious emergency, that allowed Charles more control over taxation. He was able to levy the *aides* without summoning assemblies, through officers appointed by the crown, and thereafter this became the custom. In 1439, a further estates general at Orleans voted a *taille* for defence. The effect of these reforms was cumulative, and the real benefits came when the English were driven out of France, but the crown continued to be able to levy taxation. However, together with loans from his wealthier subjects, these fiscal reforms did improve royal income sufficiently for Charles to feel no further need to summon the estates general (Potter, 2002. pp.177–8).

taxation.
Charles VII
as threat
to English

In contrast to Wolfe, Potter argues that Charles's reign did not mark a radical departure in royal policy towards the estates. Far from being the norm, the crown only summoned estates as an emergency measure. Charles was therefore really re-establishing and improving a system that was already in place before his reign (Potter, 2002, pp. 172–8). Graeme Small, in turn, argued that the decline of the estates was not uniform. While the estates general became much less frequent (the last was summoned in 1440), some provincial or local estates continued to meet, either to grant taxes to the king, or to their local ruler (as in Brittany, Burgundy and Auvergne), or performed other useful administrative functions (Small, 2003, p. 152–3).

Charles's financial reforms did play a significant part in helping him to defeat the English, however, because they enabled him to pay and discipline his troops. In the 1420s and 1430s Charles had relied mainly on mercenary troops raised by individual captains and great nobles. Their loyalty could be suspect, and when their wages were unpaid (a common occurrence given the crown's financial weakness), soldiers lived off the countryside, virtually holding it to ransom. By the 1430s and 1440s, taxation probably seemed a lesser evil to Charles's subjects than being subjected to 'friendly troops' laying waste their region, to enemy attack, or to the crown's stop-gap measures to raise money (such as manipulating the currency).

Charles introduced a series of reforms in the 1430s and 1440s to improve his armies and discipline the soldiery. The ordinance on the *taille* of 1439 (see above) also forbade the raising of private armies. From 1445 to 1448, Charles reorganised his army from a largely noble cavalry to regular companies of mounted men at arms and archers, which could serve him either in the field or in garrisons in towns. He got rid of the majority of captains, integrating the remainder into the ordinance companies, more stable units in the royal army: the *Grande Ordonnance* or great ordinance company (cavalry) and the *Petite Ordonnance* or lesser ordinance company, that was stationed in garrisons to protect the frontiers (Guenée, 1985, p. 142). He purchased artillery, which was essential for siege warfare. The king was therefore able to equip and pay a more powerful army than his nobles could, giving him another source of patronage for loyal servants, such as military posts for the nobility. A regular income from taxation was not spent only on military measures: it also enabled the king to pay pensions to the nobility, and the running costs of his court and administration.

Some historians have seen the developments of Charles VII's reign as a stage in the transition from a 'judicial' state, where royal power rested on the king's right to administer justice throughout his kingdom outside his domain, to a 'fiscal state', where the crown's power rested on the ability to raise large sums of taxation throughout the kingdom (Potter, 1995, p. 136). It has also been viewed as part of a broader European trend stretching from the medieval to the modern period, whereby rulers gradually gained a monopoly of armed force within their principalities.

Contemporaries, however, feared the king's power would encourage him to act as a tyrant, able to levy taxation at will and impose his wishes by the use of armed force. Were they right? Although Charles could raise about 1.8 million livres by the end of his reign, the average tax burden may have been little changed from a century before. It became much heavier under Louis XI, though, reaching a peak of almost 5 million livres (see Table 1.2).

Table 1.2 **Average wages of a master mason (a skilled building worker) in Normandy, from the mid fourteenth century to the late fifteenth century**[8]

	Date		
	Mid 14th to mid 15th centuries	***c.*1461 (death of Charles VII)**	**1483 (under Louis XI)**
Days' wages required to pay taxes (based on an average working year of 240 days	24	26	69

Furthermore, Charles VII's reforms did not mean the crown had absolute power to levy taxation at will. The *taille* was only levied directly by royal officers in three-fifths of the kingdom: elsewhere (in Brittany and Burgundy) regional representative estates continued to meet and vote the taxes.

Even where estates declined, this can be seen as a stage in the long tradition of negotiation between the crown and local communities; the crown granted privileges in return for something from the beneficiary. In the 1420s, Charles had bargained with his regional estates (as Henry VI's government had increasingly to do with the Norman estates in the 1430s and 1440s). While in the north, the *aides* were levied at a standard rate from the 1430s, the estates in the south were granted the power to vote a lump sum or 'equivalent' to the king, instead.

When grants of taxation no longer came through the estates, local communities found other ways to negotiate. P.S. Lewis argued that the estates had actually *complicated* proceedings, and that towns, for example, really preferred to strike their bargains with, and pay sweeteners to, 'fixers' – influential nobles or officers who could promote their clients' interest with the king (Lewis, 1981, pp. 31–50), rather than compete with all their rivals for concessions through the estates.

Another example of bargaining can be seen in a royal ordinance on the *taille* (November 1439) that prohibited lords from levying *tailles* on free men, rather than unfree tenants. This is often cited as an example of the way the crown asserted a monopoly on taxation at the expense of the nobility. In fact, the ordinance also confirmed noble *exemption* from taxation, which had been gradually evolving over the previous century, on the principle that the nobility defended the king in person in battle (and were therefore already making a contribution to defence).

Exemption from taxation can in fact be seen as part of the same process of bargaining. It was one of the many privileges enjoyed by individuals and communities in later medieval France that was granted, or tolerated by, the

---

[8] Based on estimates by Contamine (1992, p. 128) and Bois (1984, p. 105). The fragmented nature of the records means that extreme caution is needed when using these figures.

crown. In addition to the nobility, clergy were exempt, although they did make separate grants to the king. Royal officers and urban elites enjoyed exemption because they granted loans and gifts to the king, which gave him cash in hand (whereas taxes could only be collected slowly). The growth in exemption had important political, economic and social consequences that lasted beyond Charles's reign, for the tax burden fell increasingly on the less prosperous in towns and in the countryside.

Charles VII introduced significant financial and military reforms. However, it can be argued that his reign witnessed a restoration in royal power rather than a new departure. Charles's reign can be seen in the longer-term context in which the crown had to bargain with individuals and communities for support, in return for the grant of privileges, rather than as part of an inexorable trend to absolute royal power.

The nobility

> Alas! Sire, I don't wish at all to say that your relatives don't behave well and loyally towards you; but there is amongst them a very considerable amount of envy, which causes a number of troubles ... Send them against the enemy and find a way of paying them ... This is what the good king Charles [V] your ancestor used to do; for he had none of his brothers near him and when they came to see him he used to give them some thousand écus to go back again.
>
> (Jean Juvénal des Ursins, treatise addressed to Charles VII, 1440, cited by Lewis, 1968, p. 127)

Jean Juvénal sums up here the ambivalent relationship between king and nobility, particularly the king's close relatives. The nobility were a relatively small group (between 1 and 2 per cent of the population), but they enjoyed political and social importance out of proportion to their numbers. The greatest nobles, including the duke of Burgundy, were closely related to the king, and potentially were in the line of succession to the crown, but their rivalries for a share of royal patronage and wealth could also cause conflict and even civil war.

At its best, the relationship between crown and nobility could enhance royal power – France was too big for the king to rule alone. The greatest nobles had a network of followers in their lordships. Access to royal favour gave them a source of patronage and therefore influence over their followers. Historians refer to this type of relationship as 'patronage and clientage', based on a noble's protection and grant of material favours to an equal or an inferior in return for that individual's loyalty and various other services. This was gradually replacing an older relationship, known as feudalism, where a lord granted land to an inferior or vassal, who owed him services and duties in return. The king himself was the key player in this complex of relationships. Historians of medieval England employ the term 'bastard feudalism' to refer to such relationships, but very little comparative research has been done for late medieval France. Patronage and clientage could lead to instability, however: Burgundians and Armagnacs had vied to control the king, expelling each others' clients from royal offices and disrupting royal government.

Some great nobles were virtually rulers in their own right. In addition to the duke of Guyenne (who was also king of England), the count of Foix in south-west France had interests in Navarre (in Spain) as well as in France. The count of Foix claimed to rule 'by the grace of God', an implicit denial that he held his lands from the French king. Late medieval counts of Foix and Armagnac were fighting each other for control of south-west France; in some respects the Hundred Years War just seemed a cover for their private war. The conflict between France and England allowed skilful nobles, such as the duke of Brittany, to act like independent princes. The dukes of Brittany even claimed that their duchy had once been a kingdom and had a coronation ceremony at their accession (see Figure 1.11).

neighbours

This situation challenged royal claims to sovereignty in France. The existence of these princely states reminds historians that France could have become a loose assemblage of almost independent states under a weak overlord. A historian of medieval Brittany, Michael Jones, warned of the danger of 'tunnel vision' when looking at French history: that is, assuming that from its origins France was destined to develop into a strong monarchy (Jones, 2003, pp. 1–29).

How did the victory of Charles VII over Henry VI change the relationship between the king and his nobles? The great nobility had fewer opportunities to play one side off against the other. This did not stop some of them attempting to conspire with the English, or with each other (including Charles's son and heir – the dauphin and future Louis XI). Charles, however, was able to take more drastic action against rebellious nobles. In 1458, the duke of Alençon was tried and condemned to death for plotting with the English, although this sentence was commuted to imprisonment. A contemporary miniature shows Charles VII presiding in majesty at the trial, surrounded by his Parlement and nobility (see *Visual Sources*, Plate 1.2).

However, there were limits to his success. The dukes of Brittany continued to govern as virtually independent princes. In the 1440s and 1450s, in spite of the attempts of Charles's counsellors to trick them into admitting they owed liege homage (symbolising their exclusive loyalty to the king), three successive dukes insisted on giving simple (that is, not exclusive) homage. Their independence was symbolised by the fact that they paid homage standing and wearing their swords, and Charles accepted this, even making a joke about it!

The key change in the relationship between crown and nobility came in the reigns of Charles's successors, Louis XI (reigned 1461–83) and Charles VIII (reigned 1483–98), which witnessed a virtual royal take-over of some of the major fiefs within the kingdom. Louis XI took the opportunity of the death of Charles the Bold, duke of Burgundy, to seize the duchy of Burgundy, and at the death of René of Anjou he succeeded to René's lands, which included

Figure 1.11   The coronation of King Arthur of Brittany: the regal status of the duke of Brittany, as seen by a late-fifteenth-century Breton chronicler, Pierre Le Baud and the artist of the manuscript. Paris, Bibliothèque nationale de France, Paris, FR 8266. Photo: Bibliothèque nationale de France, Paris

Anjou and Provence (the latter was not technically part of France). Charles VIII forced Anne, duchess of Brittany, to marry him; after his death her marriage to his successor Louis XII kept the duchy in the crown's control. These acquisitions not only removed some of the king's most powerful rivals, but added to the royal domain. Nonetheless, this development has to be seen in a wider context stretching beyond our period. Many of these lands were subsequently granted out, while the nobility continued to be a powerful force in the kingdom well beyond our period, and in the sixteenth century played a key role in a new set of civil wars, known as the Wars of Religion, between Catholics and Protestants.

The royal administration

> In all you do have regard for the good [of the king] in whose service you are ... sustaining his rights and the public good [chose publique].
> (Jean Juvénal II des Ursins, archbishop of Rheims, treatise to his brother, the chancellor of France, 1452)

When we try to assess the impact of the royal administration, we have to bear in mind that France was a large country (contemporaries estimated it as 22 days' journey from north to south and 16 days' journey from east to west). Communications were poor by modern western European standards. Paris, the seat of the main royal institutions, was a fortnight's journey away from Carcassonne in the south.

Charles VII recognised these difficulties. Although he merged his administration with that in Paris after 1436, it was more important for him to administer justice effectively to his subjects than to protect the position of Paris as an administrative capital. Charles VII therefore kept the Parlement of Toulouse, set up in 1420, and gave other regions their own law courts or parlements, a trend that continued into the sixteenth century. This institutional decentralisation did not necessarily reduce the *authority* of the crown, reminding us that the medieval view of administration was different from the modern one (Guenée, 1981 pp. 116–25).

In spite of contemporary pleas to the king to reduce the 'multitude of royal officers and their wages', even in the early sixteenth century, royal officers accounted for only about 0.4 per cent of the population (compared with an estimated noble population of 1–2 per cent). The royal administration had originally developed to enforce royal rights, collect and audit royal finances, and administer royal justice. They were just one section of an army of bureaucrats serving the church, towns and princes, and often competed among themselves to advance their employers' power and increase their own income.

Jean Juvénal II implies that royal officers should serve the state, but they were very different from the modern image of a civil servant. The granting of offices was a way that the king could reward his servants when it was difficult for him to give them land or pensions. Officers were often poorly paid, so they sought or accepted presents of money or goods in return for using their influence.

Offices could become hereditary and pass from father to son (or son-in-law). They could be sold and purchased (that is, they were *venal*). Certain offices could confer nobility, thus contributing to the growth of a new social class: the 'nobility of the robe'. Offices therefore brought the holders prestige and profit, even though they were serving the state. The tendency for royal officers to intermarry, and use their position in royal service to gain patronage for their relatives, led to another characteristic of the late medieval and early modern state: the establishment of virtual dynasties of royal servants, with tentacles spreading through the state and the church. You will find one good example for Charles VII's reign in the Juvénal des Ursins family (see box).

Royal officers were a convenient target for criticism. Jean Juvénal himself recorded how some encouraged the king to take all the taxes he desired from his subjects, and to increase the number of posts, so that even a clerk's clerk would get his cut. 'Thinking more of greed and advancement than to fulfil their duties', officers in the parlement were slackers, preferring their own or their friends' business to the king's. 'God grant that those who serve you may be as attentive to the common good as they are to their own advantage', he wrote in a treatise addressed to the king in 1452 (Daly, 2000b, p. 102).

The historian David Potter has argued that the 'leading characteristic of public power from 1450 onwards was perhaps that of the royal office' (Potter, 1995, p. xii). But developments in Charles VII's reign were once again part of a longer-term trend. For example, sale of offices only became a royal prerogative, and an important source of income for the crown, in the sixteenth century. Under Charles VII, venality benefited private individuals. Office alone did not confer the right to ennoblement, although many *individual* officers were ennobled by the king, or enjoyed one of the privileges which became *associated* with nobility in the course of the fifteenth and sixteenth centuries: exemption from the *taille*.

The Juvénal family

The Juvénals are an excellent example of a family that suffered when the Burgundians seized Paris in 1418 (see *Visual Sources*, Plate 1.3). An account of their troubles is given in a contemporary narrative source, a history of France known as the *Chronicle of Jean Juvénal II des Ursins*. It was once thought that **Jean Juvénal II** (*c*.1388–1473), who became archbishop of Rheims, composed this text, but it is now believed to have been written for him.

> The entry into Paris by the duke of Burgundy's men was terrible and cruel, for several were dead and killed, nevertheless many important people were saved, from the Parlement ... as well as the citizens, by finding a way to leave Paris, abandoning everything. Afterwards their wives and children, by various devices, found ways to follow them.
>
> How piteous [was] among others Messire Jean Juvénal des Ursins, lord of Traînel, who possessed 2,000 livres worth of rents and income, and owned fine places and houses in France, Brie and

Champagne, with a town mansion of which the furnishings might have been worth 15,000–16,000 écus altogether: with a lady of worth and title as his wife, and eleven children, seven sons and four daughters, with four sons in law! To have lost everything, and his wife and children left barefoot, dressed up like poor people, like many others who had also lived worthily and honourably.

Before their flight from Paris, **Jean Juvénal I des Ursins**, baron of Traînel, had been a royal advocate in the Paris Parlement; his wife, Michelle de Vitry was the daughter of a counsellor there. They followed the dauphin to Poitiers, so their fortunes were linked with the future Charles VII. Jean Juvénal I was made one of the presidents in the Parlement of Poitiers by 11 January 1419, and was made president of the newly constituted Parlement of Toulouse in 1420. Two of his sons began their careers in the Parlement of Poitiers, before rising to the highest offices in church and state. Jean Juvénal II was successively bishop of Beauvais and Laon, then, from 1449 till his death, archbishop of Rheims, and **Guillaume** (see Figure 1.12) was made chancellor of France (the highest secular office in the kingdom) by Charles VII in 1445 (Lewis, 1992, pp. 27, 34–5, 43–5). They owed their rise to legal training and royal office, not noble blood. The family set up their own chapel in Notre Dame cathedral in Paris (see Anthology Document 1.8).

As bishop of Beauvais, Jean Juvénal II had been on the front line between the English and the French and the experience resulted in a collection of political writings addressed to the king. When his brother Guillaume was appointed chancellor, he sent him a treatise advising him how he should carry out his duties. Guillaume was knighted in 1428 and was baron of Traînel, and he emphasised his noble status as well as his royal office. On his tomb (which has not survived, but which we know of from a seventeenth-century drawing), and in a magnificent manuscript made after his appointment as chancellor in 1447, Guillaume was depicted as both chancellor and knight (see *Visual Sources*, Plate 1.4).

His coat of arms is also prominent on a portrait by Jean Fouquet (which probably formed part of a diptych, or two-winged, devotional painting), which shows him half length, in sumptuous clothes within a gilded décor, which the artist has emphasised.

A royal servant as consumer: Jacques Coeur

We shall now look at another type of royal servant. Jacques Coeur was a financier and merchant, and held office as treasurer to the royal household. He invested his wealth in a magnificent mansion in his home town of Bourges. In modern terms, we could think of Jacques Coeur as an excellent example of a consumer, and thus we can explore another course theme: producers and consumers. We shall see how we can use his mansion as historical evidence.

Figure 1.12   Portrait of Guillaume Juvénal des Ursins. Panel painting by Jean Fouquet. Louvre, Paris. Guillaume's coat of arms, supported by two little bears or 'oursins' (a pun on his name), is visible on the pillars to the left and right. Louvre, Paris. Photo: © RMN / © Christian Jean

---

DVD exercise

Please put on DVD 1, Jaques Coeur's Mansion. You will also need Anthology Documents 1.9–1.11, and the *Media Guide* as you watch the DVD

Summary

The development of the French state took place over several centuries. It is therefore difficult to single out factors that apply only to the period 1415–61. However, Charles VII's financial and military reforms placed greater resources in the hands of the monarchy: the *taille*, in particular, became one of the most important taxes of the early modern state. These resources allowed him to defeat Henry VI, become a focus of patronage for the nobility and ultimately reunite the divided French state. Charles's exile south of the Loire may have reinforced the links between southern France and the monarchy. The experience of war against the English may also have reinforced a sense of common identity among the French, though this coexisted with strong regional sentiments that royal government recognised and even reinforced.

> France in 1461 was not yet a united monarchical state ... [but] the mould from which the ancien regime was to be cast was in part created as a direct consequence of the war with the English.
>
> (Vale, 1998, p. 407)

The following exercise helps you to carry out a review of the unit.

EXERCISE

Look back at the characteristics of the state. Note down the extent to which, in your opinion, the state in France at the end of Charles VII's reign fulfils those criteria. It may help you to note down your results as a table.

Spend about 30 minutes on this exercise.

SPECIMEN ANSWER

	Notes
Territory and sovereignty	Expulsion of the English (except from Calais) Some expansion of royal domain Royal claims to supreme power in France Exaltation of royal power above the nobility with some success (Alençon, Foix) but with some limitations (Brittany)
Sense of common identity	Some shared views about the monarchy's image (even when France divided) Importance of regional loyalties (e.g. Normandy, Brittany)

Powers (military, judicial, and financial)	Principles of royal monopoly established (to raise *taille*, raise an army) Military reforms (but absorbs nobility rather than reduces their power) Taxation without estates but with local bargaining Decentralisation of some royal institutions (e.g. parlements)
Administration in state service	United after civil wars and Anglo-Burgundian regime Not in crown's exclusive control (sale and inheritance of office limits crown's power to appoint or dismiss) Small numbers of royal servants

CONCLUSION

In this unit, we have seen that the struggle between Charles VII and Henry VI links up with all three course themes. We have explored the relationship between the formation of the state and beliefs and ideologies about the monarchy and national identity. We have also considered examples of consumers in state service (Guillaume Juvénal and, above all, Jacques Coeur). We shall be continuing to look at these themes in Unit 2, which will include a more theoretical analysis of the historical problem of state formation.

REFERENCES

Allmand, C.T. (1983) *Lancastrian Normandy: The History of a Medieval Occupation 1415–50*, Oxford, Clarendon Press.

Autrand, F. (1969) 'Offices et officiers royaux en France sous Charles VI', *Revue historique*, vol. 242, pp. 285–338.

Beaune, C. (1985) *Naissance de la Nation France*, Paris, Gallimard. [English version Beaune, C. (1991) *The Birth of an Ideology: Myths and Symbols in Late Medieval France* (trans. S.R. Huston, ed. F.L. Cheyette), Berkeley, University of California Press.]

Bois, G. (1984) *The Crisis of Feudalism. Economy and Society in Eastern Normandy c.1300–1550*, Cambridge, Cambridge University Press.

Contamine, P. (1992a) 'La "France anglaise" au XVe siècle. Mirage ou réalité?' in *Des pouvoirs en France 1300–1500*, Paris, Presses de l'École normale supérieure, pp. 99–108.

Contamine, P. (1992b) 'Guerre, fiscalité royale et économie en France (deuxième moitié du XVe siècle)' in *Des pouvoirs en France*, Presses de l'Ecole normale supérieure, Paris, pp. 123–30.

Daly, K. (2000a) 'Centre, power and periphery in late medieval historical writing: some reflections' in Allmand, C.T. (ed.) *War, Government and Power in Late Medieval France*, Liverpool, Liverpool University Press.

Daly, K. (2000b) 'Private vice, public service? Civil service and *chose publique* in fifteenth century France' in Curry, A. and Matthew, E. (ed.) *Concepts and Patterns of Service in the Later Middle Ages*, Woodbridge, Boydell Press, pp. 99–118.

Guenée, B. (1981) *Politique et histoire au moyen âge*, Paris, Publications de la Sorbonne.

Guenée, B. (1985) *States and Rulers in Later Medieval Europe,* Oxford, Blackwell.

Jones, M. (2003) 'Tradition, history and the French: a case of tunnel vision', inaugural lecture, University of Nottingham, in Jones, M. (2003) *Between France and England. Politics, Power and Society in Late Medieval Brittany*, Aldershot, Variorum reprints, pp. 1–29.

Lewis, P.S. (1968) *Later Medieval France: The Polity*, London, Macmillan.

Lewis, P.S. (1981) 'The centre, the periphery, and the problem of power distribution in later medieval France' in Highfield, J. and Jeffs, R. (eds) *The Crown and Local Communities in England and France in the Fifteenth Century*, Gloucester, Alan Sutton, pp. 32–50.

Lewis, P.S. (1992) *Écrits politiques de Jean Juvénal des Ursins*, vol. 3, *La Vie et l'Oeuvre*, Paris, Société de l'Histoire de France.

Lorentz, P. and Comblen-Sonkes, M. (2001) *Le Musée du Louvre, Paris*. 2 vols, Paris (*Corpus de la peinture des anciens Pays-Bas méridionaux et de la principauté de Liège au quinzième siècle*, vol. 19).

McKenna, J.W. (1965) 'Henry VI of England and the Dual Monarchy: aspects of royal political propaganda, 1422–1432', *Journal of the Warburg and Courtauld Institutes*, vol. 28, pp. 145–62.

Mirouer historial abregié de France (1451) Oxford, Bodleian Library ms Bodley 968, f. 219.

O'Meara, C.F. (2001) *Monarchy and Consent: The Coronation Book of Charles V of France*, London, Harvey Miller.

Potter, D. (1995) *A History of France, 1460–1560. The Emergence of a Nation State*, London, Macmillan.

Potter, D. (ed.) (2002) *France in the Later Middle Ages*, Oxford, Oxford University Press.

Shakespeare, W. (1968) *Henry V* (ed. A.R. Humphreys), London, Penguin.

Small, G. (2003) 'Crown and provinces in the fifteenth century' in Potter, *France in the Later Middle Ages*, pp. 130–54.

Thiébaut, D., Lorentz, P. and Martin, F.-R. (2004) *Primitifs français. Découvertes et récouvertes*, Paris, Réunion des musées nationaux.

Thompson, G.L. (1991) *Paris and its People under English Rule. The Anglo-Burgundian Regime 1420–1436*, Oxford, Clarendon Press.

Vale, M. (1974) *Charles VII*, London, Eyre Methuen.

Vale, M. (1998) 'France at the end of the Hundred Years War' in Allmand, C. T. (ed.) *New Cambridge Medieval History*, vol. 7, *c.1415–c.1500*, Cambridge, Cambridge University Press, pp. 394–407.

Warner, M. (1991) *Joan of Arc: the Image of Female Heroism*, London, Vintage.

Wolfe, M. (1972) *The Fiscal System of Renaissance France*, New Haven, Yale University Press.

Kathleen Daly

INTRODUCTION

At that time [about 1465] the subjects of the house of Burgundy were very rich because of the long peace which they had enjoyed and the great moderation of the prince under whom they lived, who taxed his subjects little. It seems to me that then his territories could well have been described as the Promised Land, more so than any others on earth. They were overflowing with wealth and they had a peace which they have not since experienced in the last twenty-three years. Men and women spent free[ly] and wore extravagant clothes. The parties and banquets were more lavish and more prodigal than anything I have experienced anywhere else; there were even bathing parties and other great entertainments with women of a disorderly and often immodest kind: I speak of women of low condition. All in all, it seemed to the subjects of this house that no prince was great enough for them or was capable of reducing them to powerlessness. But today I do not know in this world a people so desolate, and I fear that the sins of the time of their prosperity have brought them their present adversity; most of all because they did not recognise that all these favours came from God who distributes them as it pleases him.

(de Commynes, 1972 [c.1489–98], pp. 64–5)

Philippe de Commynes had served at the Burgundian court from 1464 to 1472. At that stage, the lands ruled by his masters, Philip the Good and Charles the Bold, stretched across what are now France, Belgium, the Netherlands and Luxemburg, and included some of the largest and wealthiest cities in western Europe. By the time he was writing his *Memoirs* in France (c.1489–98), what was left of the Burgundian lands was only slowly recovering from nearly two decades of invasion and civil war. Commynes was not alone in seeing the final years of Philip the Good (d.1467) as a golden age, but he saw immorality and pride as causes of the downfall of the 'promised lands'. Historians, however, have debated whether this assortment of territories, with different traditions, languages and customs, could ever have developed into a state on the model of England or France.

In this unit we shall:

- look at the historical events leading to the rise and fall of Valois Burgundy
- explore the debate on whether or not Burgundy constituted a state
- consider how ducal power and wealth was displayed, and for what purposes.

Figure 2.1   A bathhouse (*c.*1470), a contemporary reflection on immorality illustrating a classical text: illustration by a Flemish artist of a French translation of the *Deeds and Sayings of the Romans* by Valerius Maximus. Handschriftenabteilung, Staatsbibliothek zu Berlin – Preussischer Kulturbesitz / Dep Breslau 2, Vol. 2, f. 244 r. Photo: BPK, Berlin / Ruth Schacht

Table 2.1 Valois and Hapsburg rulers of Burgundy

The Valois dukes of Burgundy
Philip the Bold (d.1404)
John the Fearless (1404–19)
Philip the Good (1419–67)
Charles the Bold (1467–77)

The Hapsburg rulers
Mary, duchess of Burgundy (1477–82), married Maximilian, king of the Romans.
Maximilian (1482–94) as regent for his son Philip
Philip the Fair (1482–1506), son of Mary and Maximilian, married Joanna the Mad of Castile
Charles V, king of Spain and Holy Roman Emperor (duke of Burgundy from 1506)

BETWEEN FRANCE AND THE EMPIRE: THE RISE AND FALL OF VALOIS BURGUNDY

Now turn to Figure 2.2, a map of the Burgundian lands in the fifteenth century and Table 2.1. You will find it helpful to refer to the map as you read this section.

Unlike France, the different territories ruled by the dukes had no tradition of government by a single prince. They were gradually united under four dukes, who were closely related to the Valois dynasty of kings of France. Some historians have even coined the phrase 'Valois Burgundy' to describe the lands ruled by the dukes from the late fourteenth century to 1477. The first Valois duke was Philip the Bold, brother of Charles V, king of France, who united his southern French duchy of Burgundy with the northern possessions of one of the wealthiest heiresses in Europe, Margaret of Male. Margaret, daughter of the count of Flanders, brought not only her own lands, but dynastic claims to neighbouring territories ruled by her relatives. When her father, Count Louis, died in 1384, Margaret and Philip inherited the counties of Flanders and Artois in the north, and the county of Burgundy[9] in the south. Philip also purchased the county of Charolais, near Burgundy.

Philip and his successors had two allegiances: to the French king as feudal overlord for the duchy of Burgundy, Artois, Charolais and part of Flanders, and to the Holy Roman Emperor for the rest of Flanders and the county of Burgundy. As uncle to Charles VI of France, Philip the Bold had played a leading role in French royal government during the minority, then illness, of Charles VI. Philip had also been able to divert a large amount of royal income to his own needs. Furthermore, Philip extended his influence in imperial lands,

---

[9] The county of Burgundy was also known as the Franche-Comté, literally the 'free county'.

Figure 2.2 Burgundian lands in the fifteenth century, based on Schnerb, B. (1998) in C.T.Allmand (ed.) (1998) *The New Cambridge Medieval History*, Vol. 7, Cambridge, Cambridge University Press, map 9, p. 432

securing the recognition of his second son, Anthony, as heir to the duchy of Brabant in 1404.

At Philip the Bold's death, the most important of his territories (the duchy and county of Burgundy, and counties of Charolais, Flanders and Artois) passed to his eldest son, John the Fearless. However, John was never able to enjoy the influence his father had enjoyed in France, and his efforts to do so embroiled him in civil war. As we have seen in Unit 1, John's son Philip the Good tried to preserve his power in France by allying with the English claimants to the French throne, from 1420 to 1435.

Philip the Good

France

By the Treaty of Arras (1435) Philip the Good (see Figure 2.3) abandoned the English alliance and recognised Charles VII as king of France. The duke gained important territorial concessions from Charles, which were to influence his own and his successor's policies towards France. He was given control of vital areas on the northern Franco–Burgundian border: the county of Ponthieu, the Somme towns (including Amiens, St-Quentin and Corbie) and three lordships in Picardy (Roye, Péronne and Montdidier). He also acquired the counties of Auxerre and Mâcon (see Figure 2.2).

EXERCISE

Now read Anthology Document 1.12, an extract from the Treaty of Arras. What major concession did Charles VII make to Philip? In the light of your work in Unit 1, why do you think this may have been important to Philip?

Spend no more than 10 minutes on this exercise.

SPECIMEN ANSWER

Philip is excused from paying homage and 'faith' to Charles VII. The document specifies that he is therefore exempted from a range of royal powers in lands held of the French king (such as the king's right to summon judicial appeals from ducal lands to the royal courts). This situation is limited to their lifetimes – it does not bind their successors. Philip the Good is therefore an outstanding example of a territorial prince who developed his power at the expense of the crown.

Although the extract here only refers generally to 'homage', the homage owed by the dukes to the king for the lands they held of him had traditionally been liege homage. The payment of liege homage was symbolically very important: it asserted the superiority of the lord who received the homage over the person who gave it. It was supposed to secure exclusive loyalty. It was a symbol of the superior lord's feudal power – the recipient acknowledged that he held his lands by permission of his overlord. In Unit 1 we saw the reluctance of dukes of Brittany to pay liege homage to the French king.

Figure 2.3   Duke Philip the Good. Panel painting attributed to Rogier van der Weyden, *c* 1450, oil on wood, 31 x 23 cm, Musée des Beaux-Arts, Dijon. Photo: © RMN / © Droits réservés

The empire

Philip the Good continued to see himself as a French prince, as we shall see. But the great territorial expansion in his reign took place not in France, but in the empire, with his acquisition of Hainault, Holland and Zeeland (1425–28), Brabant (1430) and Luxemburg (1443). In 1448, Philip and the emperor Frederick III had even discussed the idea of giving the duke a royal title and kingdom (to be called the kingdom either of Frisia or of Brabant), to be based on the imperial territories held by the duke. As with the Treaty of Arras, however, Philip wished to hold these lands without paying homage – in this case, to the emperor – and Frederick III would not agree. Although he remained a duke, the area ruled by Philip by 1467 was as large as the contemporary kingdom of England with Wales, though smaller than France (Vaughan, 1975, p. 23).

The late Paul Kendall: 'Louis XI : The Universal Spider' (1971)

Charles the Bold

calls him "Charles The Rash"

France

Charles the Bold's policy towards France was probably influenced by his fear that Charles VII's successor, Louis XI (ruled 1461–83), would take back the Somme towns and lordships in Picardy, the important buffer zone that Burgundy had acquired at the Treaty of Arras. The death first of Charles VII (1461) and then of Philip the Good himself (1467) threatened to undermine the independence that Burgundy had claimed since the treaty. Louis XI feared the new duke's financial and military power, as Charles the Bold (see Figure 2.4) allied with Louis's enemies in France, the English, or both, threatening to encircle France. For example, Charles played an important part in a major noble coalition against Louis in 1465–67 (the 'War of the Public Weal'). In 1468, Charles married Margaret of York, sister of the English king Edward IV, and in 1474, Edward and Charles agreed that, if Edward invaded France and became king, Edward would give Charles substantial lands in France. In turn, Louis XI tried to ally with Charles's enemies whenever he could. Between 1465 and 1477, Charles and Louis were in a state of open, or potential, warfare.

Charles took a series of measures to exclude the power of the French king, as his overlord, from his French lands. The exercise of justice was an important sign of sovereignty. The Treaty of Arras had, in theory, freed Philip's French lands from the French royal courts. However, royal administrators (particularly in the Parlement of Paris) challenged the duke's powers in his French territories, especially Flanders. On one occasion, Philip the Good was presiding over a meeting of his chivalric order, the Golden Fleece, when the parlement summoned him to Paris!

In 1468, Charles tried to exclude French royal justice by forcing Louis to agree that the Parlement of Paris would have no power in the duke's French lands, but Louis later refused to accept this arrangement. In December 1473, at Thionville (Luxemburg), Charles went further, setting up his own supreme law

Figure 2.4   Charles the Bold, duke of Burgundy. From the workshop of Rogier van der Weyden, *c* 1454, oil on oak panel, Gemäldegalerie, Staatliche Museen zu Berlin, 545. Photo: BPK, Berlin / Jörg P. Anders

Style of Government

court at Malines[10] for all his northern lands. He thus cut out the Parlement of Paris, and enforced the principle that he was sovereign in judicial matters.

Now read Anthology Document 1.13. This is an extract from the ordinance that set up the parlement at Malines. It is one of a series of key reforming ordinances that set up new judicial and financial institutions in Charles's northern lands. These ordinances are also key evidence in the historical debate about whether the dukes of Burgundy intended to seek independence from the king of France.

What image of princely power is given by this ordinance?

Spend about 15 minutes on this exercise.

Charles claims a special relationship with God. This may have reminded you of the claims of the French king in Unit 1. Justice is singled out as a special characteristic and obligation of rulers.

The empire

Like his father Philip, Charles the Bold made most of his territorial gains in the empire. He acquired Upper Alsace in payment for a loan to its ruler (1469). He confiscated the duchy of Guelders from its duke in 1473, and conquered the duchy of Lorraine in 1475.

Charles also expanded his power by intervening in the affairs of imperial bishoprics (such as Liège and Cologne), and neighbouring principalities to the south (such as the duchy of Savoy). Charles seems to have been more interested in a royal title, based on his imperial lands, than his father had been, and may even have hoped to be elected emperor himself. In autumn 1473, Charles met the emperor Frederick III at the imperial city of Trier. The splendour of the Burgundian duke's entourage impressed onlookers; at least one mistakenly thought the magnificent hat that Charles wore was a crown (see Figure 2.5). In the event, the emperor decamped in haste. But the failure of these negotiations, ironically, may have inspired Charles to set up his new parlement, to assert his status as a potential king. His conquest of Lorraine and other imperial territories may also have been intended to force the emperor's hand and make him concede a royal title (Vaughan 2002b, pp. 140–55).

Finance

Charles's ambitious policies were supported by the extensive financial resources of his Burgundian lands. Under both Philip the Good and Charles, income from the duke's own lands (or domain) was dwarfed by the income from taxation, particularly indirect taxes or aids; just as in France, taxation formed the main part of royal income. Taxes were granted to the dukes by the representative assemblies (estates) of their separate territories, and the Four Members of Flanders, an assembly representing the three great cities of Ghent,

---

[10] Also known as Mechelen, now part of Belgium.

Bruges and Ypres, and the rural area known as the Franc de Bruges. As in France, the clergy and nobility were exempt, and commoners (the third estate) bore the brunt of taxation. In 1471, Charles the Bold requested a subsidy from the estates general of all his northern lands, to establish a permanent army. By 1474–75, taxation had almost tripled, compared with Philip the Good's time, and may have amounted to two-thirds of what the king of France could collect in 1470: that is, before the enormous growth in tax revenues that marked the end of Louis XI's reign (Brown, 2001, p. 11; Garnier, 1997, p. 976). Charles's income at this time probably put him on the same level as Edward IV of England (Blockmans and Prevenier, 1999, p. 147).

Military power

As in France, the costs of war help to explain the growth in taxation. The bulk of the army consisted of the dukes' paid vassals, who brought their own contingents of archers, crossbowmen and swordsmen, supplemented by mercenaries (from England and, after 1472, from Italy) and contingents from towns. Charles the Bold introduced a series of important military reforms, designed to make his army more effective. Between 1473 and 1476, he set up permanent squadrons of cavalry, imitating those set up by Charles VII in France known as the *compagnies d'ordonnance*. He introduced a tight chain of command under the captains (*conducteurs*) of these squadrons. He imposed systematic training and rules of moral conduct on his soldiers, such as a ban on blasphemy, women and dice playing. Charles was also reputed to have the finest artillery in Europe. However, Burgundian armies throughout the period probably numbered only 5,000–10,000. They were smaller than those of the Swiss and their allies, who defeated them in key battles in 1476–77 (Vaughan, 1975, pp. 123–4), and smaller than French royal armies.

The 'grave digger' of Burgundy?

Burgundian expansion, however, had its disadvantages. Ducal lands spanned a geographical area of 500 miles from north to south, and it could take a week to communicate between the capitals of the duchies of Brabant (Brussels) and Burgundy (Dijon). These frontiers were vulnerable to the king of France, but also to enemies and rivals from the empire. A thirty-mile gap separated northern and southern ducal territories, even after the conquest of Lorraine. Charles's warlike policies can in part be explained by his desire to keep open his lines of communication and to allow mercenaries recruited in Italy to join his armies (Vaughan, 1975, pp.14–23, 187).

Charles's military ventures generally brought success until about 1474, when he suffered a series of important and expensive defeats. His interference in the archbishopric of Cologne, and particularly his siege of the town of Neuss, brought the emperor against him at the head of an army, and Charles withdrew. His expansion in Upper Alsace alarmed the powerful Rhineland cities, such as Strasburg, and the duke of Austria. He also threatened the interests of Berne, a key city in the Swiss Confederation, 'the system of alliances among imperial provinces and cities in the area between the Alps, the Jura and the Rhine' which by 1460 had 'risen to be the most important political [power] between the Rhine and the Alps' (Sablonier, 1998, p. 663).

In 1476, the Swiss and their allies defeated Charles at Grandson and Morat (near Lake Neuchâtel in modern Switzerland), a key strategic area where Charles and Berne were competing for influence. Charles had to abandon his baggage train, with valuable plate, jewels and tapestries (see box). In the same year, he had to face a revolt in Lorraine. On 5 January 1477, while besieging Nancy, the capital of Lorraine, Charles was killed by a combined army of his enemies, the dukes of Lorraine and Austria, the Rhineland towns and volunteers from the Swiss Confederation. Charles's corpse was so mangled that he was only recognised by his long nails and battle scars.

Was Charles the Bold the 'founder' or the 'grave digger' of the Burgundian state (Contamine, 1992, pp. 87–98)? After the defeats of 1476, Charles was faced with financial crisis; the estates were refusing to pay taxes (which may remind you of the last days of English Normandy, in Unit 1), and his subjects were refusing to fulfil their military service. Vaughan, however, argued that the financial machinery continued to function, and, had Charles survived, it was robust enough for him to have recovered (Vaughan, 2002b, p. 415).

The magnificent hat shown in Figure 2.5 was one of several made for Charles the Bold. It was part of the baggage abandoned to his enemies at the battle of Grandson in 1476, when the duke and his army were routed. It should have been pooled with other spoils from the battle, and divided between the allies in the Swiss Confederation. However, when it came into the hands of the city council of Basle, they kept it hidden and sold it to the Fuggers, Augsburg bankers, for 5,600 gulden in 1506. The Fuggers in turn sold it to Charles's son-in-law, Emperor Maximilian, for 22,000 gulden. The hat no longer survives. We know of its existence from a description and illustration in a sixteenth-century German work (the *Ehrenspiegel*) praising the house of Hapsburg, which was written on the instructions of Jakob Fugger. The description tells us that the hat was decorated with circles of pearls, a large ruby and two large jewelled feathers. The engraving reproduced here was made for a seventeenth-century edition of the text, following the earlier illustration (Deuchler, 1963, p. 118). Charles's goldsmith, Gerard Loyet, was paid for making other, similar hats (see Anthology Document 1.14), which Charles wore on ceremonial occasions, such as his meeting with Emperor Frederick III at Trier.

From Valois to Hapsburg

Charles's death left his lands vulnerable to his enemies. He actually had an adult heiress, his daughter Mary (see Figure 2.6), but Louis XI, king of France, discounted Mary's claims. Louis argued that the duchy of Burgundy, in particular, was a royal apanage and that, at the death of Charles, the last direct male heir, his French lands should revert to the crown. Louis seized the duchy of Burgundy and invaded the counties of Burgundy, Flanders and Artois (even

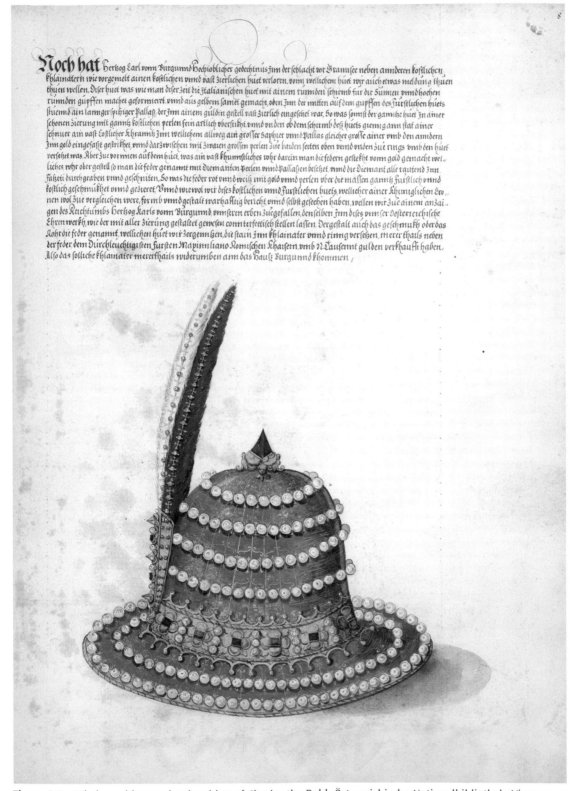

Figure 2.5   Missing evidence: the ducal hat of Charles the Bold. Österreichische Nationalbibliothek, Vienna, Cod. Vindob. 8614, f. 8 r. Photo: Austrian National Library, Picture Archives, Vienna

though the county of Burgundy and part of Flanders were imperial land). Louis was able to exploit discontent in some of the major cities in Flanders (such as Ghent) and supported their rebellion against Mary.

Mary first had to appease the discontents aroused by the harsh government of her father. She convened the estates general, and, in response to their grievances, issued the Great Privilege on 11 February 1477. This abolished many of Charles's centralising measures, gave the estates general more representation in government, and protected local customs and privileges: the 'first constitution for the whole of the Low Countries' (Blockmans and Prevenier 1999, pp. 197–8).With the support of her step-mother, Margaret of York, Mary then revived the idea of an imperial marriage, which had already been discussed in 1473 at Trier. In 1477, she married Maximilian of Hapsburg, archduke of Austria, which saved her from being forced into a French marriage, as Louis XI had planned. Mary died in 1482; Maximilian and Louis signed the second Treaty of Arras. This recognised Philip the Fair (born in 1478) as Mary's successor, while his sister, Margaret of Austria, was to marry Louis's son (the future Charles VIII) and some of the disputed lands (Artois and the county of Burgundy) were to become part of her dowry. The succession was secure. The Valois ducal dynasty had now merged with that of the Hapsburgs. However, Maximilian was not accepted as regent, as Mary had wished, leading to a renewed series of revolts. Peace was restored only in 1492, and from 1492 to 1494 Maximilian set about revoking the grants made in the Great Privilege.

Margaret of Austria never married Charles VIII (he married Anne of Brittany instead, securing that duchy for the French crown). In 1493, the Treaty of Senlis confirmed Hapsburg possession of Artois and the county of Burgundy, but the Hapsburgs promised not to take the duchy of Burgundy by force. In fact, they never recovered the duchy. However, Philip the Fair's son, Charles, ruled not only the remaining Burgundian lands, but also the kingdoms of Spain and their colonies in the New World. He was elected Holy Roman Emperor as Charles V in 1519.

Was the Valois house of Burgundy therefore resurrected with even greater powers? Up to a point. On the negative side, the axis of power moved away from the former heartland of the Burgundian 'state', that is, the duchy of Burgundy (now in French hands), and from Flanders, Holland and Brabant, to Spain and Austria – the Hapsburg heartlands. On the other hand, the traditions of Valois ducal rule (and particularly the court) influenced their Hapsburg successors. The Hapsburg emperor Charles V, Charles the Bold's great-grandson, never fully accepted the loss of the duchy of Burgundy. He asked for his heart to be buried in the Carthusian monastery founded in Dijon by his ancestor Philip the Bold (see the genealogy – Figure I.1 in the Block Introduction – and Figure 2.7).

Figure 2.6   Mary of Burgundy, fifteenth century, oil on panel, Musée Condé, Chantilly, France. Photo: Lauros / Giraudon / Bridgeman Art Library

Was there a 'Burgundian state?

We have already seen that much depends on how we define the term 'state'. You are now going to consider the views of one historian of Burgundy – Andrew Brown. This extract is part of a longer discussion on the nature of Burgundian ducal power. This is a complex article, so do not be concerned if you do not understand it all at first reading. You will have an opportunity to read it again at the end of the unit.

EXERCISE

Now read Brown, *Valois dukes of Burgundy*, in the secondary sources. As you read, note down answers to the following questions.

1   What difficulties do historians encounter when they try to define the term 'state'?

Figure 2.7   Philip the Bold (d.1404): sculpture from the ruined Carthusian monastery, or Charterhouse, of Champmol, near Dijon, France, built by Philip the Bold (d.1404), where Valois dukes of Burgundy were buried. Photo: © Image State / Hachette Photos / Hervé Champollion / TOP

2   How does Brown define 'state'?

3   In Brown's view, to what extent does Burgundy qualify as a 'state'? You may find it helpful to draw up a table with two columns: one showing Brown's definitions, the other listing the extent to which, in Brown's view, Burgundy fits or does not fit those criteria.

Spend no more than 30 minutes on this exercise.

SPECIMEN ANSWER

1   Brown points out the pitfalls of using the term 'state' without a careful definition. He notes that the perspectives of an historian's own time can affect their interpretation of the term. A unified state is not the only possible model for government either in medieval or modern times; Brown mentions the alternative example of 'federal' states.

2   Some of Brown's criteria are clearly related to modern ideas of the state: sovereignty (i.e. independence from an external power); territorial unity (both geographical and administrative); and a sense of common identity. He also discusses the 'theatre state', an idea derived from the anthropologist Clifford Geertz. 'Theatre-state' could imply that even ceremonial events were attempts at 'state formation' (e.g. entries into towns, particularly after rebellions).

3   Brown's ideas are summarised in the table below.

Criteria	Burgundian dukes
Sovereignty/independence	Though neither duke held a royal title, both Philip the Good and Charles the Bold took measures to make the lands they held from the French king more independent of royal control. Both dukes tried to increase their landholdings within the empire, where their overlord was weaker
Unitary territory / centralised government	There was never a single kingdom comprising the northern and southern territories, and the dukes never succeeded in uniting their lands into a single continuous territorial bloc. The Valois rulers held each land under a different title (duke, count, lord, etc.). They did attempt some general administrative measures, for example taxation (from 1435) on a more general scale, while Charles the Bold established a parlement at Malines (although this dealt only with his northern lands)
Identity	Philip the Good tried to develop a sense of identity: among the nobility, through the chivalric order of the Knights of the Golden Fleece, and through association with gilds and processions in towns. This was probably jeopardised by Charles the Bold's policies, but survived his death, though the king of France kept the duchy of Burgundy. The Hapsburgs revived organs of ducal government and the Golden Fleece. However, even at its most successful, effective ducal rule was reliant on 'considerable negotiation with urban subjects'

Ant. doc. 1.13

1.17(c)

1.18

1.19

1.20

When revising the block, you may find it helpful to review Unit 1 in the light of Brown's criteria.

POWER AND CONSUMPTION

When reading the extract from Brown, you may have noted how historians have seen visual splendour as an important aspect of ducal power and prestige. At Trier, in 1473, Charles's Burgundian courtiers drew unflattering comparisons between the poor table manners of Emperor Frederick III's attendants and the splendour and order around the duke. Their attitude shows the importance to contemporaries of the ruler's image and wealth. Material possessions and ceremonies could be used to impress the dukes' actual and potential allies, and overawe their enemies. The magnificence of the ducal court, the chivalric order of the Golden Fleece, and ducal patronage of craftsmen, writers and other artists far outshone the court of the Lancastrian English kings and the royal courts of France.

For the rest of this unit we shall be exploring how the way the dukes spent their income may have enhanced their power and affected the nature of the late medieval Burgundian state. This will link our exploration of the state with our theme of producers and consumers.

Life at court

EXERCISE

Read the first two extracts from Éléanore de Poitiers' treatise on how to behave at court (Anthology Documents 1.15a and 1.15b); this is an important source on ideas about status and ceremonial in the fifteenth century. When reading, jot down a response to the following questions.

1   What can we learn from the first extract about the behaviour required of the nobility, in Éléanore's opinion?

2   What can we learn from the second extract about the impression the ducal household and court made on contemporaries?

Spend no more than 30 minutes on this exercise.

SPECIMEN ANSWER

1   Ceremonious behaviour is used as visual evidence of an individual's birth, honour and status. You may have singled out such gestures as the holding of a lady's train, curtseys, whether an individual is held by her right hand (the position of honour) or the left (honourable, but less so) ... . It is often difficult for historians to penetrate the exact meanings and nuances of this elaborate ceremonial. However, the duchess of Burgundy's behaviour is a visible sign that she acknowledges the superior social status of the French king, his queen, the dauphin and the dauphin's wife. On the other hand, the way that they treat the duchess demonstrates her superiority to other princesses. Ceremonial was not necessarily clear cut, witness the competition between the duchess Isabel and the Queen of Sicily over their relative status.

2   In the second extract, you may have been struck by the wealth on display at the birth of Mary of Burgundy, particularly if you think the birth of a baby is a private event for family members.

I have not reproduced all of Éléanore's description, which dwells in great detail on the way the room was draped in rich cloths and tapestries, and on its public nature. The duchess expected to be visited in her bedroom or chamber by members of the court and visiting dignitaries. At the time of Mary's birth, her father (the future Charles the Bold) had not yet become duke, but he was the heir apparent, and the birth of his daughter was an important event with serious political consequences.

Now look at *Visual Sources*, Plate 2.1 – a visual representation of a court. We have to use the image with caution because it is not a direct illustration of *Burgundian* court life, but of a story (a chivalric romance). Nevertheless, it does help us to visualise how wealth was displayed at court. There is a dresser, or buffet, displaying costly plate. It is worth noting that silver and gold plate was often melted down and used to pay troops (one of the reasons why so little plate survives from the period) or pawned to get ready cash to pay troops.

In the same image, we can see a procession of household officers serving the prince. Éléanore's third extract in Anthology Document 1.15, on how inferiors must not usurp privileges that should belong only to great nobles and princes, alerts us to the significance of what we might consider quite minor distinctions (whether bread is broken or cut at the table, whether the noble officer carries a napkin over his shoulder or his arm, and so on). Are there any clues in the procession to the status of the officers' master (or mistress?).

'Court' and 'household'

So far we have referred to 'court' and household' without really distinguishing them. What do these terms mean? They have caused some disagreement among historians. I have been following Malcolm Vale's broad definition of the court. This fits the court of the Burgundian dukes, even though Vale was studying the courts of the fourteenth century.

According to Vale, the court was where the ruler was: 'the prince's environment, both a place, normally of unfixed location, and an assemblage of people' (Vale, 2001, p. 31). The Burgundian ducal court was not fixed in one place but was peripatetic: that is, it moved from one ducal residence to another. The dukes had palaces throughout their territories: at Hesdin in Artois, at Dijon in the duchy of Burgundy, at the Prinsenhof at Bruges, and at the Coudenberg in Brussels. This mobility was characteristic of late medieval courts throughout Europe.

The household provided the 'framework for the court'. It consisted of those who met the material needs of medieval rulers 'below stairs', mainly non-noble, and the politically powerful who held ceremonial and political offices around the ruler 'upstairs'. Looked on as a group of people, rather than as institutions, the court and household served comparable functions, and both provided important meeting places for the prince and his subjects (Vale, 2001, pp. 22–31).

Historians, sources and the Burgundian court

Why have historians been so interested in the Burgundian court? It is partly because of the outstanding source material, unparalleled for medieval Europe (Paravicini, 1991, p. 88). In addition to accounts of ceremonies at court and in the household by Éléanore de Poitiers (Anthology Document 1.15) and Olivier de la Marche (Anthology Document 1.16) we also have a series of ordinances describing the personnel and the daily records of expenditure for the material life of the household (wages, purchases of food and other items, travel and so on), which are still being studied by historians. Compare this with a 'virtual blank' in the records for Lancastrian English kings, although more material survives for the reign of Edward IV (Starkey, 1999, p. 1). The situation is little better for France for this period, although some of the few remaining fragments have been exploited (notably by Vale, 1974, pp. 217–22). Historians of these countries try to understand such fragmentary evidence by exploring parallels with the Burgundian court (possibly overestimating Burgundian influence in the process).

Does the survival of so much source material give us a misleading image of the importance of the Burgundian court and household? The fact that the dukes were willing to spend so much, and so many of their subjects were willing to serve there, shows their importance. According to the calculations of Blockmans and Prevenier (1999, p. 148), in 1445 the ducal household absorbed 32 per cent – almost a third – of the duke's recorded income. It grew in size throughout the period: from 234 office holders in 1426 under Philip the Good to 1030 under Charles in 1474 (Paravicini, 1991, p. 76). The Burgundian dukes also created a system whereby offices rotated: that is, household officers would serve at particular times of year ('service by term'). This increased ducal patronage, as there were more offices for the duke to award to the nobility of his territories. Charles the Bold drew very heavily on his household for captains for his army.

The importance of court and household is borne out by the impression they made on neighbouring rulers. Olivier de la Marche's account of the household (Anthology Document 1.16) was intended as a model for Edward IV of England, and was later copied for Charles the Bold's Hapsburg successors. The court was the setting for splendid feasts and court pageants, such as the Vow of the Pheasant in 1454, when a figure dressed as the church begged Philip and his subjects to rescue her from the Turks. This was a reference to the fall of the eastern limit of Christendom, the great city of Constantinople (modern Istanbul), which was captured by the Turks in 1453. Philip and many of his nobles took a vow to go on crusade against the Turks. This enhanced his image as a Christian ruler.

To understand why the dukes spent so much on their household and courts, and why subjects and contemporaries were impressed, we need to look more closely at what happened there and who attended. Whereas administrative institutions (such as the chambre des comptes, or chamber of accounts) were separate from the household and court, the 'nucleus of power, political rule, remained in the hands of the court' (Paravicini, 1991, p. 86).

Ducal service could bring subjects many advantages and related perks, such as presents, access to ducal favour, pensions, ennoblement or promotion to a higher status within the nobility than they had been born to. Some officers, such as the governors or lieutenants of territories ruled by the dukes, were consistently recruited from the ranks of the nobility (Vaughan, 1975, p. 84). As in France, commoners could also gain wealth and status (for example, the ducal chancellor Nicolas Rolin). All could seek favours and offices for their network of relatives, vassals and followers (or clients) attracted to their service: that is, the group known to historians as their affinity. Office was something to be competed for; this was often to the prince's benefit, but such competition could also cause severe disruption at court (See Anthology Document 1.17).

The perils and rewards of office: Chancellor Rolin

'It is he who organises everything, and through whose hands ... everything passes', the mayor of Dijon wrote in 1443 (Schnerb, 1998, p. 443). Nicolas Rolin (born between 1376 and 1380, died 1462) provides an outstanding example of the career open to a really successful ducal official. He came from a family of burgesses and lawyers in Autun in ducal Burgundy (part of the kingdom of France). Nicolas himself was a counsellor in the Parlement of Paris, but served the Burgundians, unlike the Juvénals who were Armagnacs (see Unit 1). Duke John the Fearless appointed Nicolas one of his counsellors. Philip the Good appointed him chancellor in 1422, when Nicolas was in his 40s. He was the highest ranking officer in the ducal administration and the best paid, receiving an annual income of 25,000 livres. He was knighted in 1423, and over his lifetime he accumulated lands worthy of a high-ranking ducal official. Nicolas's international influence was reflected in his son Jean's appointment by the pope as bishop of Chalon, then Autun, and finally, in 1449, as a cardinal.

Nicolas's power brought him enemies at court, and his career was ended by a dispute with his rivals, the Croys, over a court office. Charles, count of Charolais (the future Charles the Bold) wanted Anthoine Rolin, another of Nicolas's sons, to be appointed to a post in Charles's household, but Duke Philip favoured Philippe de Croy, lord of Sempy. The Croys had originally been a minor noble family with lands in France and Picardy. However, like the Rolins, they had flourished in ducal service. Anthoine de Croy was governor of Luxemburg, Namur and Boulogne, while his brother Jean (Philippe de Croy's father) was captain-general and high bailiff of Hainault. The Croys had alienated some of the greatest nobles in their rise to power, and their enemies – led by the duke's own son – supported Anthoine Rolin (Vaughan, 2002a, pp. 337–9). Matters came to a head on 17 January 1457, in a scene described by

[handwritten annotations:] e Ghent Altarpiece" (1425-32)

Jan van Eyck (c.1390-1441) born in Maaseyck; north of Maastricht d. Bruges

May 1425- appointed painter to Philip the Good.

Jewel-like perfection + 3/4 faces

Figure 2.8 *Chancellor Rolin in Prayer before the Virgin and Child*, by Jan van Eyck, fifteenth century, oil on wood, 66 x 62 cm, Louvre, Paris. Photo: © RMN / © Hervé Lewandowski *[handwritten:] (c.1435)*

Chastelain (see Anthology Document 1.17b) that reminds us that life at the Burgundian court was not as orderly as commentators such as Éléanore de Poitiers might lead us to believe. The Rolins lost: Anthoine did not get the post and Nicolas was forced to give up the chancellorship. Furthermore, even Charles of Charolais was virtually excluded from power for the next seven years. Nicolas died in 1462, aged in his 80s.

Figure 2.9 The Hôtel-Dieu, Beaune, France, 1853, engraving by F. Bedford after Henry Clutton. Photo: Hulton Archive / Getty Images

Rogier van der Weyden (c.1399–1464) b. Tournai, Belgium d. Brussels

c.1436 – appointed painter to the city of Brussels

A contemporary chronicler, Jacques du Clercq, noted that 'the said chancellor was reputed one of the wise men of the kingdom, concerning temporal matters – as for the spiritual, I shall keep quiet' (Comblen-Sonkes and Lorentz, 1995, p. 22). However, Rolin left his mark as a patron of outstanding religious works of art, particularly a panel painting showing the chancellor in prayer before the Virgin and Child by Jan van Eyck (see Figure 2.8). Rolin and his third wife, Guigonne de Salins, an aristocrat from the county of Burgundy, founded one of the outstanding examples of Burgundian architecture of the fifteenth century – the Hôtel-Dieu, or hospital, at Beaune, where they were later buried (Figure 2.9). It contains a striking painting of the *Last Judgement* by another great artist, Rogier van der Weyden (Visual Sources, Plate 2.2).

Anthology Document 1.17, taken from the court chronicler George Chastelain, gives a slightly different view of the ducal court, which is worth comparing with that of Éléanore. Chastelain is quite critical of some of the ceremonial carried out at Charles the Bold's court, which, he suggests, alienated the onlookers rather than impressed them. In this respect, he seems to be drawing an implicit contrast with Philip the Good.

van der Weyden (although not court painter) painted the most popular portraits (not Van Eyck)

BRABANT

BURGUNDY (PHILIP I)

SAXONY

THURINGIA

BURGUNDY (PHILIP II)

BRUNSWICK

FOIX ?

(4)

ARAGON ?
(Descended from PHILIP III ×
ISABEL of ARAGON 1262

Figure 2.10 Jean Wauquelin presents Philip the Good with the romance of Girart de Roussillon, illuminated manuscript painting from Girart de Roussilon, Österreichische Nationalbibliothek, Vienna, Cod 2549 f. 6 r. Photo: Picture Archives, Austrian National Library, Vienna

Was there a change in the way the prince's image was represented between Philip the Good and Charles the Bold? This is much more difficult to decide.

Look at *Visual Sources*, Plate 2.3 (*The Military Ordinances of Charles the Bold*, 1473). You should also look at Anthology Document 1.16, which is a description by Olivier de la Marche of the ceremony in which Charles appointed his captains of the ordinance. This copy was prepared for Charles himself, and this manuscript was made in 1475.

How is Charles the Bold represented? What image do you think the duke is trying to convey?

Spend about 20 minutes on this exercise.

In the miniature, Charles is represented seated on a throne, under a canopy (or dais), a mark of his high status (Éléanore de Poitiers singled out canopies as one item those of inferior status should not have). Charles is placed centrally in the miniature, raised above his captains, who kneel to receive their batons and books of ordinances. He is handing a baton to a kneeling figure (one of the newly appointed captains). The rest of the court watch the proceedings. The miniature is surrounded by shields that depict Charles's different territories.

Was this a new departure? This depends on which images of Philip the Good we look at. Plate 2.4 in the *Visual Sources* gives us one view of Philip, surrounded by his officers and nobles, which became a very influential model for images of the duke. However, we can find other images of Philip that are more similar to this one of his son (see Figure 2.10). Éléanore's recollections of the court under Philip the Good, though written much later, also indicate Philip's punctilious concern for ceremonial (Anthology Document 1.15). An extract from Chastelain implies that Charles was even more enthusiastic about good order than Philip (Anthology Document 1.17c). Paravicini's comparison of the court under Philip and Charles has led him to conclude, like Chastelain, that Charles set greater store on order and ceremony than did his father (Paravicini, 2000, p. 311–59).

PATRONAGE AND POWER

We have already used some of the fine manuscripts created for the Burgundian dukes as historical sources. We shall now pause to consider where such luxuries were produced.

Urban society played a crucial role. Craftsmen often learnt their trade in towns, under the supervision of a master, and were subject to the regulations imposed by trade gilds. Towns such as Bruges, Ghent, Brussels and Valenciennes also provided a market for such goods. Paintings, manuscripts, tapestries and other costly goods were exported, along with fine Flemish cloth, to Italy, England, France and other countries. Towns also played an important role in supplying the court, and the court in turn provided a market. A lucky few craftsmen, such as the artist Jan van Eyck, held a post in Philip the Good's household, and also received commissions from others at court (such as Chancellor Rolin, see Figure 2.8). More usually, the duke was one of many patrons. The artist Rogier van der Weyden (*c*.1399–1464) not only produced individual works for the duke (such as the portrait of Philip attributed to him, which we saw earlier – Figure 2.3) and courtiers, he was also town painter of Brussels, and prepared decorations for civic festivals (Kren and McKendrick, 2003, p. 90).

The market for luxury items outside the court is a fascinating subject, but one too large to tackle here. Instead we shall look at why the dukes became consumers of particular luxury items: in this case, books.

The making of many books: the ducal library

The size and splendour of the ducal library under Philip the Good and Charles the Bold set it apart from that of other contemporary rulers. Historians have studied it as evidence of the cultural interests of the dukes. They have exploited the series of inventories that were drawn up at the death of each duke (which record the possessions passed on to their heirs) to trace the development of the collection. Payments in the ducal accounts also provide valuable information about the artists and authors of books commissioned by the dukes. Fortunately, nearly half the books inventoried in 1467 still survive in public and private collections across the world. They have generally fared better than other works of art, such as the magnificent Carthusian monastery near Dijon – the Charterhouse of Champmol – founded by Philip the Bold but largely destroyed during the French Revolution (see Figure 2.7).

Books were a sign of the owner's magnificence and wealth. Before the later fifteenth century (and the spread of printing), hand-written books (manuscripts) took a long time to produce and were expensive. For example, the miniature of Charles the Bold with his captains (*Visual Sources*, Plate 2.3) cost 5 livres or 200 groats: the daily wage of a master-mason in the Flemish building trade at this period was about 12 groats (Kren and McKendrick, 2003, pp. 63, 252–3).

Books also contributed to a prince's image as a wise ruler. This was already apparent in the library of Philip's great-uncle, Charles V of France, who established an enormous library in the Louvre in Paris, and commissioned both original works and translations from Latin into French of political, moral, religious and historical texts. But unlike the royal collection, which was sold in 1422 (the duke of Bedford acquired the lion's share), the library of Philip the Bold and John the Fearless (amounting to some 250 volumes) passed to Philip the Good. By his own death, in 1467, he more than tripled the collection to 867 volumes, most of which he acquired in later life, from about 1445, when he became 'the most active manuscript collector of his dynasty and possibly of his time' (Blockmans, 1998, p. 8).

How can we use the library as evidence? In his analysis of the books acquired by Philip the Good, Blockmans identified several important trends. First, he showed that only sixty manuscripts were definitely commissioned by Philip: in these, payment appears in the ducal accounts, or there is evidence of his ownership in the manuscript (for example, a presentation scene, inscription, heraldry or emblems). Second, these books help us draw conclusions about ducal interests. In Philip's library, texts with a moral purpose (such as books of conduct or mirrors of princes), religious works (including breviaries and books of hours), and historical works are the most numerous. Third, Philip seems to have been prepared to spend most money on large illuminated books of history (of about 14 × 30 centimetres), suggesting that he valued these especially. Why was this?

Making the past, making the present: history and the dukes of Burgundy

We have already seen that Philip ruled different territories. He was often one of a number of claimants (and not always the most popular). Thus he had needed the recognition of the representative assembly, or estates, of Brabant, to succeed to that duchy, even though the previous duke had been his cousin. In return, he had had to swear to maintain the Brabanters' extensive privileges. His succession as count was also contested in Holland, Hainault and Zeeland, where he had to enforce his claims with an army.

Rulers, however, could use the past to justify their claims to political power. History included not only what we would term 'historical' figures, but also those who we would consider mythical, or whose story had been so embroidered that little of what we think of as historical 'fact' – supported by documents or other evidence – remained. For example, Plate 2.4 in the *Visual Sources* shows Philip being presented with the *Chronicles of Hainault* by Jean Wauquelin. Wauquelin had translated some existing Latin histories of the county to show that Philip's claim to rule legitimately could be traced back to the earliest rulers (and for which, by modern standards, there was no historical evidence).

Figure 2.10 shows the same author (Jean Wauquelin) presenting Philip the Good with the romance of Girart de Roussillon. Girart was a ninth-century ruler of the principality of Lotharingia, which by the fifteenth century was identified with some of the lands ruled by the Burgundian dukes. A fourteenth-century poem describing Girart's chivalric exploits and battles with his overlord, the Carolingian king Charles the Bald, was turned into prose at the Burgundian court, where it provided historical justification for Philip's own disputes with the current French king, Charles VII.

Other works produced for Philip were based much more closely on what we would term historical fact. Edmond de Dynter, a ducal secretary of Brabant from 1406 to 1448, included over 300 references to, or extracts from, archival documents in his Latin chronicle of the dukes of Brabant, which he presented to Philip in 1447. However, Dynter also included a series of genealogies to prove that Philip was both more closely related to previous rulers, and had a better right to rule, than rival claimants to the duchy. History and politics were therefore closely linked. Dynter's Latin text was translated into French on Philip's command in the same year.

Blockmans explains Philip's interest in political terms:

Philip's historiographical commissions obviously sought to legitimise his political claims to an ancient descent and a sovereign position as the heir ... In this respect their extraordinary format and lavish illumination served a clear purpose.

(Blockmans, 1998, p. 15)

PART 2

Philip was clearly aware of the value of historical writing to promote a favourable image of his rule: he was the first duke to appoint an official Burgundian chronicler, George Chastelain (see Anthology Document 1.17), a practice later followed by Charles the Bold. We need to be aware, nevertheless, that the initiative did not always come from the duke, as the quotation from Blockmans implies. Wauquelin undertook the *Chronicles of Hainault* at the initiative of Simon Nockart, a ducal counsellor in Hainault, although the duke then took a keen interest and paid a large sum for them to be illustrated. Dynter undertook his chronicles on his own initiative, evidence that Philip's subjects wanted to teach the duke about the history of the regions he had come to govern (Small, 2000, pp. 17–22).

Historians have argued that the interaction between the dukes and their noble subjects is also reflected in wider cultural change under the last Valois and early Hapsburg dukes. An elite of nobles, active at court, serving the duke in his lands, often members of the dukes' chivalric order, the Golden Fleece, adopted the tastes of the dukes for prose romances and historical works. These works were written in French, the language spoken by the dukes, rather than Latin, the learned language of the church, or Dutch, which was spoken by a large number of the dukes' northern subjects. This cultural development was most striking in Holland and Flanders, where in the previous generation, books owned by the great nobility had been in early Dutch or German, and had been moralising or practical texts (Wijsman, 2003, pp. 19–37). It has been described as a process of 'Burgundianisation', in which common cultural interests linked the duke and his most powerful subjects, and has been compared to the way that powerful and previously independent princes were drawn into ducal service through pensions, offices and election to the Golden Fleece.

Charles the Bold did not live long enough to accumulate a library like his father. However, Olivier de la Marche described how, after an exhausting day, Charles the Bold would retire to his private chamber, where close companions – the squires of his chamber – entertained him: 'some sang, some read romances and others spoke of love and arms' (la Marche, 1883–88 [1475], vol. 4, p. 16). Both dukes were also interested in the classical past. However, Charles took a special interest in the deeds of military heroes such as Julius Caesar, Hannibal and Alexander the Great, whose stories featured in his manuscripts and on tapestries (see Figure 2.11 and Anthology Document 1.20). He emulated their military success.   *"Golden Fleece" as a consequence of this.*

We have looked at the interests of the consumers: let us end with the producers. Ducal patronage may have helped authors gain a wider audience for their work and new patrons, before and after the arrival of the printing press. An illustration (not included here) in Philip the Good's *Chronicles of Hainault*

Figure 2.11   Tapestry: the triumph of Julius Caesar (Tournai, 1465–70). This tapestry may originally have been made for Charles the Bold's throne-room, but now has the arms of his lord chamberlain Guillaume de la Beaume. Photo: Historisches Museum Bern

actually shows a book being read aloud in duke Philip's presence – a good way of arousing readers' interest in the years before book prizes.

The duke and his subjects

> Burgundian power was something of a syndicate in which people took stakes so as to share in the fortunes of the house.
>
> (C.A.J. Armstrong, cited in Small, 2002, p. xii)

The dukes of Burgundy could not govern alone. In practice, they needed the support of key groups of subjects. In Unit 4, you will be learning something about the relationship of the dukes with the church. In this unit, we shall look at examples of ducal interaction with the nobility, through the Golden Fleece, and relationships with powerful towns, taking as a case study ducal relations with the town of Ghent, in Flanders. We have chosen these examples because they show how display and ceremonial could be used to enhance ducal power, and therefore the way that consumption could be used in the service of the state.

The duke and the nobility

We have seen that from the 1440s the dukes ruled a wide variety of territories. Historians have emphasised ways in which key political groups, such as the nobility, became partners in ducal government rather than rivals to the duke. As we have also seen, the court was a key element in this process. More generally, it was in the dukes' interests to attract nobles into their service, and for the nobility to enjoy ducal favour, as the balance of power, and income, shifted towards the dukes. The dukes tried to stop the nobility building up their own affinities, at least in Flanders, while using pensions to encourage members of the nobility who could be useful to them into their service (Armstrong, 1983, pp. 215, 226). Even before the dukes acquired the county of Hainault, the important de Lalaing family received money-fiefs. Money-fiefs required the recipient to pay liege homage (see Unit 1), implying a closer bond of loyalty than a mere pension would bring, and allowed him to display the ducal arms. Charles the Bold tried a similar policy in Guelders. By allowing nobles to take one-third of the aides levied from their tenants by the duke, Philip secured their cooperation, just as the dukes themselves, as vassals of the king of France, received a share of royal taxation levied in their French fiefs.

Historians have also investigated the way ideals such as chivalry, as well as material means, could be used to build common interests between the dukes and their most powerful subjects.

The Golden Fleece

The Golden Fleece was a chivalric order founded by Philip the Good on 10 January 1430, during the celebrations for his marriage to Isabella, daughter of the king of Portugal. Chivalry (*chevalerie* in French) was an idealised code of conduct for knights which developed from about the twelfth century. It emphasised courage in battle, loyalty to one's lord, protection of the weak (orphans, widows) and Christianity. Chivalric orders such as the Golden Fleece embodied the chivalric values that a ruler and his nobles shared, and were supposed to display, principally in battle (and above all on crusades against non-Christians) but also in the jousts and tournaments that were popular in the later Middle Ages. Orders of chivalry were common in later medieval Europe: the Order of the Garter had been instituted by the English king Edward III as early as 1348. In fact, George Chastelain explained the foundation of the Golden Fleece by Philip as a tactful way of declining an offer of the Garter made by Bedford, the regent of France, on behalf of Henry VI; there is no way of proving this, but it does indicate contemporary awareness of the political significance of these chivalric orders.

The order was socially exclusive: only the great nobility could become members of the Golden Fleece. Originally just twenty-four knights were admitted (including Anthoine de Croy, whom we met above), though this was later increased to thirty-one. They had to be legitimate and both their parents and grandparents had to be nobles. However, the Golden Fleece was geographically inclusive, with members from the whole range of Philip's territories. The order was also given an appropriate (though legendary) origin: a mixture of the classical myth of the Golden Fleece found by Jason and the Argonauts, the biblical story of the fleece used by Gideon, and a good dose of chivalric romance. It was also given its own historian, to record its members' prowess in combat for posterity.

EXERCISE

In the light of what you have just read, look at Anthology Document 1.18, the statutes of the chivalric order of the Golden Fleece. As you are reading, note down:

1   the purpose for which the order was founded, according to the statutes;

2   how the order may have enhanced the dukes' power.

Spend about 20 minutes on this exercise.

SPECIMEN ANSWER

1   Philip wanted to foster chivalry as a means of protecting the church, the Christian faith and the public good (see the introductory paragraph, or *preamble*). A great deal of emphasis is placed on fellowship between the members. This included the duke, as the statutes promise he will undertake no wars without members' advice (clause 6). We can see a combination of chivalric and religious beliefs in this purpose.

2   The duke alone is the head of the order (clause 1). We can see that the dukes originally intended members to have no other orders of chivalry, thus reducing the chance that another order (perhaps of an enemy prince) might undermine members' loyalty to the duke (clause 2), though this was later amended. The knights had to swear loyalty to the prince as head of the order and they wore a special insignia –a sheep (the fleece) suspended from a decorative collar of flints issuing sparks, the symbol or device of the Burgundian dynasty. They had to attend regular meetings or chapters, over which the duke presided, and which were held in different places within his territories (although the home of the order was in Dijon).

DISCUSSION

*For
Ghent,
see
Liège
Vaughan*

This tells us about the ideal – what was the reality? The order does seem to have reinforced the bonds between the duke and his great nobles, while emphasising ducal superiority. Knights are shown around the dukes in illustrations in ducal manuscripts (*Visual Sources*, Plates 2.3 and 2.4) and the order was celebrated in a ducal entry into Ghent in 1458. The knights surrounded their ruler at important occasions, such as Charles's revocation of the privileges of the city of Ghent at Brussels in 1469 (Anthology Document 1.20) and his meeting with Frederick III at Trier (Vaughan 2002b, p. 146). They accompanied him into battle and led his ordinance companies. On the other hand, the offer of the collar of the Golden Fleece to a foreign prince (allowed in later versions of the Statutes) might be used to reinforce an alliance with a foreign ruler. (See Figures 2.3 and 2.4 for illustrations of the dukes wearing the collar of the Golden Fleece.)

Dukes, like other members, had to submit to a review of their activities, when colleagues reported on whether they had acted in accordance with the high standards of bravery and honour demanded by the order. For example, Charles felt called upon to give a lengthy explanation of his behaviour, although if he had not, it is unclear what action the order could, or would, have taken (Anthology Document 1.19). But membership of the order did not guarantee unswerving loyalty, particularly after the death of Charles the Bold. Charles's illegitimate brother, Anthoine de Bourgogne, entered the service of Louis XI and even joined the French king's rival chivalric order of St Michael. In fact, Anthoine refused to hand back the Golden Fleece and was never formally expelled.

The prince and the cities

In the Low Countries, towns were crucially important, both as a source of ducal wealth and as a potential focus of opposition. Towns were more numerous in Flanders, Brabant and Holland than in France or England, and more powerful (apart from Paris and London). This was thanks to their textile industry and position astride key trade routes to the Baltic and Italy. The most important source of wool for the textile industry came from England. Reliance on English wool created problems when the duke of Burgundy was at war with England (as it had for earlier counts of Flanders). There was a long tradition of urban revolt, particularly in Ghent, although the dukes were sometimes forced to bargain or even had to flee ignominiously from their cities. However, towns were often divided in themselves, with the *poorterij*, or wealthier burgesses (citizens) and the dukes in alliance, to keep order and avoid civil unrest.

The duke also added to pressures within towns. He needed more taxation and thus a more compliant municipal government. His courtiers saw a means of increasing their own influence. Both tried to take a leading share in the allocation of municipal offices, often overriding urban privileges. The urban elite, in turn, could profit by becoming clients of the duke or his courtiers.

On the other hand, the dukes also forged links with their urban subjects, as they had with the nobility. Ducal entry ceremonies allowed the dukes to meet their subjects, and the cities to draw ducal attention to their loyalty. The dukes joined urban confraternities: Philip joined the Dry Tree of Bruges, and Charles the fraternity of Our Lady of the Snow in the same city (Brown, 2001, pp. 17–18).

(handwritten: John of Gaunt, 1341, to Philippa of Hainault)

The case of Ghent *(handwritten: (historical capital of Flanders))*

(handwritten left margin:)
Edward III of England claimed French throne from Philip of Valois. To push Fl + Brab to take his side, in 1336, Edward claimed monopoly on the trade of wool

Flemish count of Nevers, took French side. Jacob van Artevelde insisted on a deal with the English. Rebellion. Philip the Bold, D of B married Margaret of Male, acquired Holland, Zeeland, Hainault and Friesland.

Where the relationship between duke and town did break down, the consequences could be spectacular. Ghent provides a particularly stark example of urban pressures in the face of ducal demands and deep social divisions. The town earned Philip's anger in 1447 because it took a leading role in opposing a ducal salt tax. Relations deteriorated as the duke tried to influence municipal elections, then the city returned councillors hostile to Philip. Ghent artisans called a strike in 1451 and in December elected three captains to replace the aldermen, who were seeking a reconciliation with the duke (Arnade, 1996, pp. 98–105). Philip had a military blockade placed round the city and eventually defeated the town's militia on 23 July 1453 at the battle of Gavere, about 13 kilometres south of Ghent. A heavy fine (840,000 pounds, the amount paid in tax by the whole county of Flanders between 1440 and 1443), was imposed on the city, though this was reduced in 1455 to 168,000 pounds (Blockmans and Prevenier, 1999, p. 127). The city had to make a humiliating submission to the duke, in a ceremony where 2,000 of its citizens, including the aldermen and captains, deans (or heads) of the gilds and others had to kneel, confess their offences and plead for forgiveness, in French (Ghenters normally spoke Dutch). The duke confiscated the banners of the gilds, which had symbolised civic resistance to his authority.

Now turn to *Visual Sources*, Plate 2.5. This image comes from a manuscript book made between 1453 (the date of the most recent document and of the battle of Gavere, also illustrated in the manuscript) and Philip's death in 1467. It shows the burgesses of Ghent making the *amende honorable* (a ceremony which, literally, 'made amends' or reparation for an offence) to Philip in 1453. The manuscript is substantial, between 300 and 400 folios long, and contains statutes and privileges granted by counts of Flanders to Ghent and the county of Flanders, between 1241 and 1453, in their original languages of Latin, Dutch and French. There are two full-page, ten half-page and three quarter-page miniatures.

EXERCISE

In previous exercises I asked you to use sources to answer a question, often involving careful description of the image, or text, and I gave you additional information to deepen your understanding of what you have studied. Here I want to turn the exercise on its head by asking you:

What key features can you identify in this miniature, and what additional information would you need to be able to interpret this image? (Where possible, I have given you the additional information in the discussion that follows the specimen answer.)

Just look at the image and make a list of the features you think are important, and what other elements need to be explained.

Spend about 30 minutes on this exercise.

DISCUSSION

1   On the left facing us we can see Philip the Good mounted on a white horse, followed by his troops, one of whom holds a pennant (flag). Who are these, what events are depicted and do we need to know what is on the pennant?

The event is generally understood to be a representation of Philip the Good. The fact that Philip is mounted emphasises his role as a knight and military leader, and also his power. The pennant helps to identify him, as it bears the ducal coat of arms and motto 'Aultre n'aray' ('I will have no other').

2   The citizens are kneeling – a sign of submission – they are also holding banners, which again we would need to identify.

The banners display the coats of arms of Flanders and the city of Ghent in chief (i.e. on top) and, in the lower half, the arms of the city gilds – only five can be clearly seen: (from left to right) candle moulders, lamb processors, wool weavers, smiths, boatmen.

3   In the background we can see a city that we need to identify.

The city in the background is actually Ghent, although the only features that have been identified convincingly are the Belfry (the tower on the right) where the city's privileges were kept.

4   The arms in the lower border need to be identified, so do the collars.

They are Philip's ducal arms, those of his wife, Isabella of Portugal (with her motto 'tant que je vive' – 'As long as I live'), and those of Charles, their son (the future duke). Philip's and Charles's arms are surrounded by collars of the chivalric order of the Golden Fleece.

5   We need to know more about who commissioned the manuscript and why.

The miniature emphasises Philip's status and power as count of Flanders and the subordination of the citizens, particularly the gilds. We might therefore assume that he commissioned it. However, there are differing views about who ordered it. It may have been Philip himself, to commemorate his victory. But why would Philip have wanted a copy of the privileges, most of which he had since withdrawn? It was more likely to have been an initiative of the citizens, made as a peace offering to the duke on his triumphal entry in 1458, in an attempt to persuade him to restore the city's privileges.

Whoever commissioned this manuscript, the ducal entry into Ghent in 1458 provides valuable context for the image of harmony and subordination presented in this miniature. To win back Philip's favour, Ghent persuaded him to make a formal entry and marked the occasion with ceremonies that stressed reconciliation; as a Ghent lawyer, Mathijs de Grootheere, told the duke:

> Because it pleases you, owing to your most blessed grace, to visit us, we rest assured that the past is over and effaced, thanks to your noble courage. We thank you as humbly as we can by offering what is ours and what is possible, namely our corporations, our goods, our wills, and whatever might please you in order to sustain you.
>
> (de Grootheere, translated by Arnade, 1996, p. 134)

Theatrical tableaux, hangings, symbols and mottoes that decorated the city were a blend of compliments to the duke, expressions of the city's submission to him, and Ghenters' view of the special importance of their city. Symbols of the Golden Fleece and the names of the order's knights were attached to one of the city gates; the Ghenters also staged the history of Gideon (a patron of the order) in the ducal palace of Ten Waale at the end of the procession. Another scene, the Paschal Lamb, symbolised Christ reconciling God and humankind. However, this scene was also an allusion to one of the city's most famous possessions, the altarpiece of the *Adoration of the Lamb* by the artist Jan van Eyck (Arnade, 1996, pp. 133–42).

It is important to note that, as in Paris (Unit 1), responsibility for, and the cost of, the celebrations lay mainly with the citizens. Gilds vied with each other to produce the most dramatic tableaux or mimes, which had their own political messages. Thus the shippers' gild constructed a tableau of a boat, decked with 431 torches and the arms of the gild combined with those of the duke. On the boat, they enacted the biblical stories of Abraham's intended sacrifice of his son Isaac, and of Moses, symbolising obedience to authority. 'The display promoted the gild's importance as much as it did Philip's honor' (Arnade, 1996, p. 140). The shippers wished to remind the duke that they had supported him when other Ghent factions had been hostile, though the submission of 1453 had treated all the citizens together as 'rebels'.

Peter Arnade has emphasised the symbolic importance of this entry for relations between the town and the duke:

> [T]he entry assured Philip of his prominence in the urban sphere and the respect and honor his urban clients owed him ... It offered (him) a near-perfect picture of urban harmony after a difficult war that had revealed the city's competing factions. It portrayed the aldermen as in control ... [and the different groups of citizens] as peaceful bodies whose self-esteem depended in part on a rivalry for the duke's favor.
>
> (Arnade, 1996, p. 142)

As in Paris, such ceremonies can give us an insight into what the ideal relationship between a ruler and the ruled should be, but cannot be taken as fact, any more than can the image in the *Privileges*. Relations between Charles the Bold and Ghent were damaged when Charles's entry into Ghent as the new duke in 1467 ended in a riot. Later, Ghent was so afraid of sharing the fate of the city of Liège, which had recently been brutally conquered by the duke, that the burgesses made a humiliating submission to the duke, and in an ostentatious ceremony symbolising his power, Charles deprived the city of most of its privileges (see Anthology Document 1.20). After Charles's death, Ghent revolted again in 1477 and played a leading role in opposing Maximilian's regency (Blockmans and Prevenier, 1999, pp. 198, 201).

CONCLUSION

Your answers to the following exercise will form the conclusion to this unit.

Now review what you have done in this unit. Give yourself time to look at the illustrations and anthology documents, particularly those that you have not read in detail as you went through the unit. While you are doing this, keep in mind the following questions.

1   How did Philip the Good and Charles the Bold try to promote their power and encourage loyalty? Were their subjects passive onlookers, or did they play an active role in the process?

2   What information in this unit could you refer to when discussing the course themes?

Your answer should be simple, a list of items you think are important with page references to help you find the same items again. I will leave this to you – I have not given a specimen answer, just a discussion.

You should spend no more than 1 hour on this exercise.

1   I would have listed the household and court, the Golden Fleece, and the projection of the ducal image through manuscript illumination and historical writing, and also brute force: the use of ducal armies against Ghent. I would suggest that there was a dialogue between the duke and his subjects, shown in competition for office and favour at court, and the ducal entries into Ghent.

Of course, this dialogue reflected the power balance at any particular time. As in France, princes tended to listen more attentively when they needed something from their subjects. But we should not underestimate the importance of 'playing by the rules': as in the case of France, subjects considered they could distinguish a just ruler from a tyrant; rulers who violated the principles of just government were threatened by rebellion on earth, and eternal damnation.

2   What you have used under one theme could be used for others as well. However, taking the theme of the formation of the state, you could use Brown's material. In the case of producers and consumers, you could refer to the dukes' wealth, and their ability to tax their subjects. You could discuss how a large percentage of this income was spent on their household. Precious artefacts (such as the plate mentioned by Éléanore de Poitiers or manuscripts in the ducal library) also impressed contemporaries. For the theme of beliefs and ideologies, you could have discussed some images and documents that projected the dukes as powerful, just or pious rulers, and showed how court ceremonial emphasised their status.

REFERENCES

Allmand, C. (ed.) (1998) *The New Cambridge Medieval History*, vol. 7, *c.1415–c.1500*, Cambridge, Cambridge University Press

Armstrong, C.A.J. (1983) 'Had the Burgundian government a policy for the nobility?' in *England, France and Burgundy in the Fifteenth Century*, London, Hambledon Press, pp. 213–36.

Arnade, P. (1996) *Realms of Ritual. Burgundian Ceremony and Civic Life in Late Medieval Ghent*, Ithaca and London, Cornell University Press.

Blockmans, W. (1998) 'Manuscript acquisition by the Burgundian court and the market for books in the fifteenth-century Netherlands' in North, M. and Ormrod, D. (eds) *Art Markets in Europe, 1400–1800*, Aldershot, Brookfield, Ashgate, pp. 7–18.

Blockmans, W. and Prevenier, W. (1999) *The Promised Lands* (trans.E. Fackelman), Philadelphia, University of Pennsylvania Press.

Brown, A. (2001) *The Valois Dukes of Burgundy*, Oxford, Davenant Press.

Comblen-Sonkes, M. and Lorentz, P. (1995) *Corpus de la peinture des anciens Pays-Bas méridionaux et de la principauté de Liège au Quinzième siècle, 17: Musée du Louvre, II*, Brussels, Centre Intérnationale d'Étude de la Peinture Médiévale des Bassins de l'Escaut et de la Meuse, Réunion des musées nationaux.

Commynes, P. de (1972 [*c.*1489–98]) *Memoirs* (trans. M. Jones), Harmondsworth, Penguin.

Contamine, P. (1992) 'Charles le Téméraire fossoyeur et/ou fondateur de l'État bourguignon?' in *Des Pouvoirs en France 1300–1500*, Paris, Presses de l'École normale supérieure, pp. 87–98.

Deuchler, F. (1963) *Die Burgunderbeute. Inventar*, Bern, Stämpfli.

Garnier, P.-L. (1997) 'Les services de la trésorerie des guerres et la recette de l'artillerie', *Revue du Nord*, vol. 79, pp. 969–91.

Kren, T. and McKendrick, S. (2003) *Illuminating the Renaissance: the Triumph of Flemish Manuscript Painting in Europe*, Los Angeles, Getty Museum/London, Royal Academy of Arts.

La Marche, O. de (1883–88 [1475]) *Mémoires* (ed. H. Beaune and J. d'Arbaumont), Paris, Société de l'Histoire de France, 4 vols, vol. 4.

Paravicini, W. (1991) 'The court of the dukes of Burgundy. A model for Europe?' in Asch, R. and Birke, A. (eds) *Princes, Patronage, and the Nobility. The Court at the Beginning of the Modern Age c.1450–1650*, London, German Historical Institute/Oxford, Oxford University Press.

Paravicini, W. (2000) 'Ordre et règle. Charles le Téméraire en ses ordonnances de l'hôtel', *Comptes rendus des séances de l'Académie des Inscriptions et Belles-Lettres 1999*, pp. 311–59.

Sablonier, R. (1998) 'The Swiss Confederation' in Allmand (1998), pp. 645–70.

Schnerb, B. (1998) 'Burgundy' in Allmand (1998), pp.431–56.

Small, G. (2000) 'Les *Chroniques de Hainaut* et les projets d'historiographie régionale en langue française à la cour de Bourgogne' in Cockshaw, P. and van den Bergen-Pantens, C. (eds) *Les chroniques de Hainaut ou les ambitions d'un prince bourguignon*, Turnhout, Brepols, pp. 17–22.

Small, G. (2002) 'Introduction' in Vaughan (2002a).

Starkey, D. (1999) 'Henry VI's old blue gown: the English court under the Lancastrians and Yorkists' in *The Court Historian*, vol. 4, part 1, pp. 1–28.

Vale, M. (1974) *Charles VII*, London, Eyre Methuen.

Vale, M. (2001) *The Princely Court: Medieval Courts and Culture in North-West Europe*, Oxford, Oxford University Press.

Vaughan, R. (1975) *Valois Burgundy*, London, Allen Lane/Penguin.

Vaughan, R. (2002a) *Philip the Good*, Woodbridge, Boydell Press.

Vaughan, R. (2002b) *Charles the Bold*, Woodbridge, Boydell Press.

Wijsman, H. (2003) 'La librairie des ducs de Bougogne et les bibliothèques de la noblesse dans les Pays-Bas (1400–1550)' in Bousmanne, B., Johan, F. and van Hoorebeeck, C. (eds) *La Librairie des ducs de Bourgogne*, Turnhout, Brepols, vol. 2, pp. 19–37.

Rosemary O'Day

INTRODUCTION

The main theme of this unit is the formation of the state. You have considered this with regard to France. Now we turn to England at the close of the French wars. We will also pay some attention to the theme of producers and consumers.

It probably seems odd to suggest that a bloody, vicious struggle in which Englishmen fought one another for control of the throne, during what has come to be called the Wars of the Roses, eventually brought about political stability and itself took place against a background of relative social harmony and economic prosperity. It will seem less strange to suggest that war against a foreign enemy had the effect of unifying the English 'state' and that that war, the Hundred Years War, had other notable consequences, while the cessation of the war left Englishmen free to quarrel among themselves. Yet both these statements form an important introduction to this unit.

WHAT HAPPENED IN ENGLAND AFTER THE HUNDRED YEARS WAR?

We begin this unit with four linked exercises designed to help you to read and use a secondary source effectively.

What functions do secondary sources (sources produced by historians) perform? Why do we need to read them? First, they can provide a coherent narrative context for the historian. Second, they may offer an up-to-the-minute interpretation of new primary sources, which includes source criticism. Third, they can involve an interpretation based on a re-examination of old themes and well-known primary sources. Fourth, they perhaps contribute to debates among historians about interpretations. Finally, they can stimulate a reader to ask new questions of the evidence.

Emphatically, *they are not substitutes for primary evidence.*

EXERCISE

Now turn to the reading by Malcolm Vale, 'The end and aftermath of the hundred years war', in the secondary sources. Don't read the essay in detail yet; step back a little and attempt to define and use this secondary source by answering the following questions on the basis of a quick examination of the introduction and conclusion to the essay.

1   What is it?

2   Does it have footnotes/endnotes and/or a bibliography/reference list?

3   What does the author set out to do? Read carefully the title and introduction
    and examine them, in order to answer this question: What is the theme of the
    chapter?

Spend about 10 minutes on this exercise.

SPECIMEN ANSWER

1   It is a chapter in a book intended for both students and scholars. It was
    published in 1994 and took account of primary and secondary sources
    discovered or produced before 1993.

2   There are some endnotes. There is a reading list but not a full bibliography of
    every book, article or contemporary source that the author consulted when
    researching and writing the essay.

3   The author does not set out to provide a chronological narrative of events. He
    provides sufficient narrative and description to make his argument clear to the
    reader. He is discussing not the impact of the Hundred Years War on England but
    the impact of what followed on from the end of the war.

DISCUSSION

Footnotes and references are important because they give the reader the
opportunity to assess the strength of the evidence employed and, should they have
the time and inclination, to do so by examining the originals.

EXERCISE

It is now time to make a brief, rough outline of the essay. Do this by scanning the
chapter briefly – skip through, reading just the first line or two of each paragraph
and note down the page on which the author begins to treat in detail the effects of
losing the French lands (you will need to return to this page for the following
exercises). Such an outline will include, as a minimum, identification of the
introduction (with relevant page numbers) of the various sections of the essay (again
with page numbers) and of the conclusion.

Spend about 15 minutes on this exercise.

SPECIMEN ANSWER

Introduction, p.

Loss of French lands, p.

Impact of loss of French lands, p.

Impact of loss of wine trade etc., p.

Relations with Europe and especially Low Countries, p.

Cultural change, p.

Conclusion, p.

EXERCISE

Now read the article more carefully and make brief notes on the following
questions:

1   What does the author set out to do?

2   What are the main arguments?

3   Taking each argument in turn, make very brief notes on the evidence the author
    uses to support his arguments.

Spend about 20 minutes on this exercise.

1   To show what impact the ending of the Hundred Years War (and the loss of the French possessions) had on English history in the later fifteenth century.

2   That the close of the war and the loss of French lands did have a profound impact (physical and psychological) on the English, but that in the long term it did not lead to English isolationism or withdrawal from Europe. Initially it strengthened the sense of national identity. The ending of trading monopolies in France forced the English to look for markets further afield. Under Edward IV, the English drew closer to Burgundy in terms of styles of government and of trade.

3   There are no footnotes but it is possible to work out from the text what evidence Vale used. For example, he used the Paston letters and other contemporary descriptions to demonstrate the close links between the English court and that of Burgundy. He used English architectural styles, glass and panel painting, and artistic patronage to show the influence of Burgundy on the arts in England (see Plate 3.2).

From your reading of this one source, what do you think were the effects on English domestic politics of the ending of the Hundred Years War, when Gascony (Aquitaine) was finally lost in 1453? Write in note form.

Spend about 15 minutes on this exercise.

• England drew in on itself at first – it was no longer a military power of the first rank. Initially, the end of the war 'enhanced existing tendencies towards a sense of national identity which had developed during the Hundred Years War'. Perhaps England became more insular and focused on making the Channel secure. Renewed alliance with Burgundy, and afterwards with the Hapsburgs, ended this insularity.

• Losing French possessions in Normandy and Gascony (Aquitaine) was a psychological shock; there was loss of prestige.

• Instability and civil war at home hindered efforts to reclaim French possessions.

• Some of those who had lost their own lands in France became disgruntled and blamed Henry VI – 'Many English knightly and gentry families were represented in Lancastrian France and had much to lose there. This had considerable bearing upon their subsequent involvement in English civil war'.

• Most of the dispossessed returned, some to support Richard of York while others remained loyal to the Lancastrian house.

• English trade monopoly and privileged position (especially in the Bordeaux wine trade) ended. This especially affected ports of west and south England, which were forced to search for new markets and supplies (in Iceland, Baltic, Spain and the Americas).

• Continuing importance of Calais – a colony of English who maintained active trade connections with the Low Countries rather than France.

• Connections with the Low Countries strengthened by renewed alliance with Burgundy, who supported the Yorkist claim. In 1468, Edward IV's sister Margaret married Charles the Bold of Burgundy. After Charles's downfall, the Austrian and Spanish Hapsburg rulers of the Low Countries saw England as a valuable ally against France.

- Cultural change – no longer predominantly French. Important Burgundian links have cultural importance – e.g. Edward IV's revived Order of the Garter emulated the Burgundian Golden Fleece and there was conscious attempt to imitate Burgundian chivalry. There are architectural, visual arts, music and literature examples too.
- This turning to the Low Countries also had its effect on domestic politics and administration.
- The court becomes the centre of power – the 'household as instrument of power and patronage was paralleled in England by the creation of a king's 'affinity' (or body of nobles and gentlemen holding household offices) at the Yorkist court'.

DISCUSSION

Vale considerably modifies the views often expressed about the consequences in England of losing the Hundred Years War. These tend to stress England coming out from under the heavy influence of France and having the chance to evolve as an English nation in terms of culture, religion, society and economy, as well as in terms of domestic politics and constitution. Vale, however, shows how England after the Hundred Years War was not culturally isolated and not politically isolationist. England remained an 'outpost of north-west Europe, linked by economic and cultural ties to the Atlantic seaboard of the Continent'. Although Vale is referring back to the effect of the Hundred Years War itself, he is more interested in offering an interpretation of developments in England during the second half of the fifteenth century – a time when other historians have concentrated on the causes and effects of the Wars of the Roses. The Low Countries replace France as the focus of English attention, and this has effects in terms of government, economy, consumption and culture.

This, therefore, is a secondary source that presents a distinctive interpretation of later fifteenth-century English history on the basis of selected primary sources.

(See Figure 3.1 for an image of William Bruges, first garter king of arms.)

EXERCISE

Vale's essay gives us some pointers to the nature of the English state. Look back through your notes and see what you can deduce about the forms of government in England in the mid to late fifteenth century. Write down your answers in brief note form.

SPECIMEN ANSWER

1   England was ruled by a king. It is a monarchy.
2   There is a parliament.
3   There is an aristocracy.
4   The king's household is important in the government.
5   Although there is civil conflict (the Wars of the Roses), this does not seem to involve an attempt to end monarchy – just to replace one king by another.
6   England almost entirely withdraws from France but does not become isolationist.

Figure 3.1   William Bruges, first garter king of arms, shown kneeling before St George. His appointment underlined the importance of the Knights of the Garter. Fifteenth century, British Library, Stowe MS 594, f.5v. Photo: The British Library

Summary

When you read any secondary source, you need to approach it systematically. Skim reading and reading topic or lead sentences are useful skills to develop. Make some brief notes as an aid to your memory – using a highlighting pen is *not* enough. Vale's essay helps us to focus on interpretations that suggest that the Hundred Years War had a long-lasting impact on developments in England. One persistent view is that, when the English were cast out of France, they became more conscious of their national identity and more isolated from Europe. Vale shows the absurdity of the second part of this proposition, adducing evidence of England's connections with the Low Countries, the Baltic and eventually the Protestant German states. The English state developed close governmental, commercial and cultural relations with other parts of Europe and turned its face away from France.

ENGLISH SOCIETY

Vale's chapter picks out some of the ways in which the English state was affected by the withdrawal from France. It withdrew, unwillingly, into its geographical boundaries but did not become isolationist. But can this be the whole story? After all, England was war-torn from the middle of the century onwards. It is important to gain some understanding of the fabric of English society in the late fourteenth and fifteenth centuries. Although by modern standards social and economic change was gradual, it helps to explain to some extent the stresses and strains to which the state was subject in the later fifteenth century, and focuses our attention on the links between two of our themes: the formation of the state, and producers and consumers.

Estates

There were three orders or estates of society – clergy formed the spiritual estate, which looked after the spiritual welfare of the people through prayer (see Figure 3.2 for another aspect of the church's role in society); then there was the knightly or noble estate, which protected land and people by arms; and finally there was the estate of the workers or labourers, who supported both the spiritual and the noble estates through their toil. This hierarchical arrangement of society was part of a Christian framework which was anti-egalitarian and anti-social mobility. 'Let each man abide in the same calling wherein he was called' were the words of the apostle St Paul in the first century CE and this quotation was frequently used to justify and preserve the status quo.

As historians such as Maurice Keen have observed, however, this had always been 'an ideal vision' of the three estates and their relation to one another. 'It never did and never could have corresponded to reality', although until around 1350 it bore a fairly close resemblance to social relations (Keen, 1990, p. 3). By the fifteenth century it no longer did.

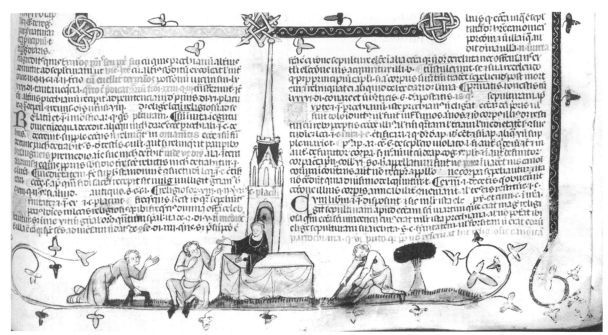

Figure 3.2 Although clergy formed a spiritual estate, they also offered succour to the poor and sick as this fourteenth-century manuscript illustrated. Decretals of Pope Gregory IX, illuminated in England, c.1330–1340. British Library, Royal MS 10 E iv, f.197. Photo: The British Library

Why had it ceased to resemble reality? At the end of the Hundred Years War with France there existed a new sense of national identity. Literacy had now spread beyond the clergy. This was still not mass literacy, of course, but enough to mean that the knightly class and the merchants could participate in literate culture; this also applied to some of the workers (see the section on Lollardy in Unit 4). The Black Death had also had profound demographic, social and economic effects, which disrupted the established relationship between the orders of society and made people question its validity.

The plague, and especially the Black Death of 1348–9 (which seems to have been a combination of bubonic and pneumonic plague), had devastating effects. Up to one-third of the population was wiped out, although the plague hit some groups and some localities more than others. For example, peasant tenants suffered greater mortality than more prosperous crown tenants, and in subdivisions (rural deaneries) of the diocese of Lincoln the death rate among clergy (a group that came into close contact with humble parishioners, whether obviously sick or in apparent health – see, for example, Figure 3.3, where the priest is performing a wedding ceremony) ranged from 28 to 60 per cent. It is extremely difficult to obtain accurate and comparable figures for the peasantry and, indeed, for the clergy elsewhere, because the records have not survived. This plague outbreak and those of 1361–2 and 1369 brought the population down to a level that, in theory, could be supported by the country's resources. However, it also resulted in an acute shortage of labour on the land, which possibly affected productivity adversely. This scarcity of labour was of long

Figure 3.3   A simple wedding blessing in front of a church. French copy of Jean de Vignay's chronicle entitled *Miroir Historial*, late fourteenth century. British Library, Lansdowne MS 1179, f. 24. Photo: The British Library

duration, probably because the plague, which hit children particularly hard, reduced the ability of the population to reproduce and recover to its old levels.

There were enormous social tensions, which are perhaps best illustrated by the reactions of the landed classes to the economic realities attendant on the Black Death and the subsequent Peasants' Revolt in 1381.

As noted above, the Black Death resulted in scarcity of labour, and especially of young strong labourers. At a time when central government intervened relatively little in the lives of subjects, and there was commensurately little central legislation, the government unusually acted to regulate the labour market in the interests of landowners. The Ordinance of Labourers (which later became a statute – act of parliament – in 1351) was an attempt to control wages and prices on a countrywide basis (setting wages and prices at their pre-plague levels) and to bind workers to their old masters (see Figure 3.4, which provides contemporary visual evidence of the work of sheep shearers, and

Figure 3.5, which shows peasants engaged in a variety of work on the land). It ordered that labourers who tried to leave their masters should be brought before the justices of the peace to be punished and sent back to their lords. This was an act that strove to protect the interests of the masters and to prevent workers exploiting the social and economic opportunities associated with a shortage of labour. It tried to preserve the social hierarchy. It seems to have been relatively effective in protecting the economic interests of landlords until the 1370s, although historians have argued that it served to harden the divisions between those who employed peasants on the land and, on the other side, craftsmen (artisans) and peasants. In 1381, there was general rebellion in Kent, Essex and East Anglia in what has come to be called the Peasants' Revolt. This was sparked by the attempt to collect an especially heavy poll tax, which was perceived to fall hardest on those least able to pay. Underlying this response to the poll tax was a deep sense that the lords had been oppressing the commons for the past three decades and also that the rulers were not protecting England against French attack. There was also an ideological undercurrent that saw the rebels demand 'freedom', abolition of serfdom and equality before the law. They wanted no lordship other than that of the king. The rebellion was quickly brought to an end in London, with minimal bloodshed, when Richard II, a boy of 14, agreed to hear the rebels' grievances, and gave the loyalists a chance to muster forces. The revolt spread into Hertfordshire, Suffolk, Norfolk, Essex and Kent but was speedily brought under control. Few of the rebels were executed.

In fact, the contemporary elite had also sought to alleviate these social tensions by making the changing social fabric fit into the pre-existing tripartite framework for social relations. Edward III's sumptuary laws (which regulated the types and colours of clothing that could be worn by differing social groups) stipulated that merchants, citizens and artisans with an annual income above £1000 could wear the same attire as an earl and those with more than £500 could wear similar clothing to esquires and lesser gentlemen. The graduated poll tax of 1379 tacitly acknowledged the emergence of other groups in society that had to be fitted into the old tripartite orders. It produced a scale of equivalencies so that, for example, lawyers, merchants and townsmen could be compared to knights and esquires (Keen, 1990, pp. 9–10). Originally knights were a military class but during the fourteenth and fifteenth centuries many merchants and lawyers became landowners and were dubbed knights. The Scrope, Fortescue and Fairfax families were some of these.

In 1381, the elite learned the lesson and no poll tax was attempted again during the Middle Ages.

A hierarchical society

Although English society was certainly hierarchical, this hierarchy was far less rigid than elsewhere in Europe: the nobility and the gentry exercised power and authority through networks of influence rather than legal rule; there existed

Figure 3.4   Early fifteenth century England was an agrarian society in which labourers such as this sheep shearer were still tied to the land. Illuminated manuscript painting. British Library, Add 17012 f.6. Photo: The Bridgeman Art Library, London

'bastard' rather than true feudalism; individuals with talent, ambition and good luck might move from one social stratum to another.

Bastard feudalism

In this society lords kept retainers: men lower on the social ladder who owed them service (including military service) and received an annual fee, livery (clothing with a badge), social standing and 'good lordship' (protection and board and lodging) in return (livery and maintenance). Anthology Document 1.23 gives two examples of indentures – the documents that sealed the contract between lord and retainer. Such liveried retainers were unpopular because they used the might of their lords to get their own way. Historians have called this relationship between lord and retainer 'bastard feudalism' because it was similar to, but not the same as, the relationship between lord and feudal tenant

Figure 3.5 A variety of agrarian occupations are shown in this painting from an illuminated manuscript from Virgil's *Georgics*, Holkham Hall, Norfolk. Photo: The Bridgeman Art Library, London

under the feudal system. In feudalism, the lord gave the feudal tenant freehold land; in bastard feudalism, the retainer was given no land, only a fee. In bastard feudalism the relationship between lord and retainer was not hereditary, as in feudalism, but for the lifetime of the retainer only, or for as long as both wished to keep the contract (Keen, 1990, pp. 19–20). Few lords kept many retainers. Exceptions included the Percys of Northumberland, who needed armed retainers to defend the border. And few retainers depended exclusively on fee income from their lord. There were also large numbers of knights and gentlemen who were not tied to a particular lord. On DVD 1, The Beauchamp Chapel, Warwick, we examine the position of the Beauchamp earls of Warwick who provide an example of the relatively rare phenomenon of a lord who dominated the locality in which he dwelt.

Remember that one of the grievances of the rebels in the Peasants Revolt of 1381 had been that it was not only the king who exercised lordship in England but also the nobility and church. In the fifteenth century, it was not only the king's authority that ran in England but also, to some extent, that of these two estates of the realm – through manorial and ecclesiastical courts, through bonds of servitude and indentures of service. The bonds that bound men and women to lords other than the king were weakened (but not ended), for example, as an indirect result of the Black Death as well as by the increasing competitive reach of the king's law throughout the land.

Bastard feudalism provided for a certain social fluidity. Lords wanted as their retainers not only loyal and deferential servants at arms but also men of talent and drive in many areas, such as estate stewardship or the law. Education could make a talented individual of humble birth as useful as or more useful than someone of good birth. Ambition could be tolerated as long as it did not threaten the interests of the lord himself. Letters relating to two 'gentry' families – the Stonors and the Pastons – can be made to yield a good deal of information about 'good lordship' and 'good mastership'. (See Figure 3.6 for a contemporary view of feasting and dancing.)

Deference

In this hierarchical society individuals were expected to both know and keep to their 'place'. They spent a good deal of time acknowledging their social inferiority to those above them (deferring) or, when they were communicating with social inferiors, making their superiority quite clear. Today we probably see modes of address and of signing off letters as mere formalities most of the time – although we still stick to certain rules. In the fifteenth century they were much more meaningful.

EXERCISE

Now read Anthology Documents 1.24 and 1.25 – letters relating to the Paston family of Norfolk and the Stonor family of Oxfordshire. Do not be put off by the unfamiliar style of the English – reading the letters aloud can sometimes help to make the sense clearer. Read the opening line and the closing line of each letter.

How do correspondents address the recipients of their letters? How do they sign themselves off? Note down examples.

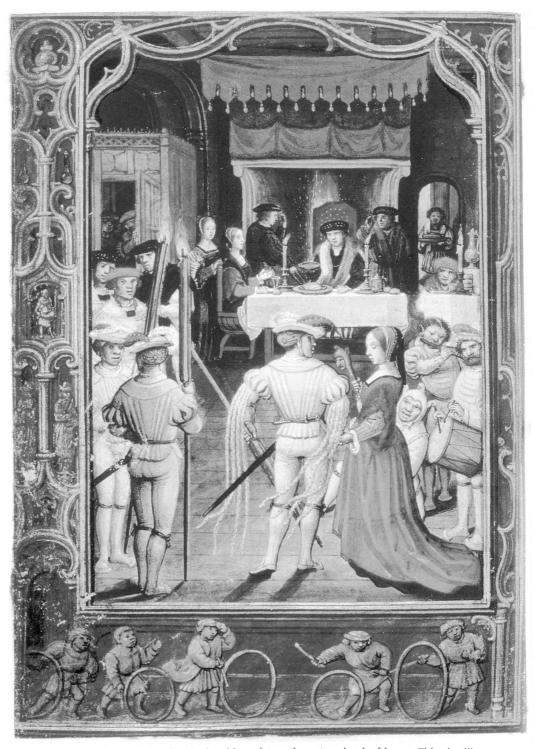

Figure 3.6   Feasting and dancing depicted in a sixteenth century book of hours. This also illustrates the hierarchical arrangement of society. The lord (probably the king in this case as he sits beneath a canopy) sits at the top table accompanied by his lady, seated to one side. The king, the queen, their noble attendants, the noble dancers are differentiated from the fool (jester), musicians, guards and servants by dress as well as by function and position. British Library, Add 24098 f.19 v. Photo: The Bridgeman Art Library, London

Spend about 20 minutes on this activity.

The opening and closing lines supply indications of deference in social relations no matter what the social position of the author – servants and apprentices deferred to masters and mistresses, business partners to senior business partners, future sons/daughters-in-law to future parents-in-law, knights to lords, suitors to their beloveds, and lords to sovereigns.

Examples of deference include these from John Paston III to his father: 'Right reverend and worshipful father, I recommend me unto you, beseeching you lowly of your blessing' and 'Your son and lowly servant'.

Family connections were eagerly claimed because then, to some extent, deference was overcome by connection. Cousinhood was used to refer to both distant relationships and sometimes even to very close ones, such as that between husband and wife. 'Right Interly and best belovyde cosyn' wrote Elizabeth Stonor to her 'hosbon' William Stonor on 9 October 1476 (Carpenter, 1996, p. 268). Deducing the precise blood relationship between two people from the mode of address is, therefore, difficult.

Letters in the Paston correspondence can be used to make similar points. I was struck, for example, by the use of the term 'good mastership' and similar phrases, even 'good brotherhood' in a letter from Clement Paston II to John Paston I, 25 August 1461 (see Anthology Document 1.24).

It is important to note that when historians refer to the knightly class or to the gentry they are not referring to a huge number of people. In Warwickshire in 1436, there were 18 knights, 59 squires and 55 gentlemen (Carpenter, 1992, p. 55). Knights were predominantly a military grouping. Almost all those noted in Warwickshire in the 1430s had served in the armies of the Hundred Years War and had been dubbed knight in recognition of their service. As a consequence, making firm distinctions between knights and gentry in terms of landholding or wealth is extraordinarily difficult.

Urban society and its relationship to the traditional hierarchical society

Our description so far is of a rural, agrarian society. Most producers and consumers were bound to the land. Towns stood awkwardly within the hierarchical structure. They were struck especially badly by the Black Death (because their population density encouraged its spread) and the shrunken populations of cities such as Lincoln and Winchester (formerly populous and prosperous) struggled throughout the fifteenth century under the burden of parliamentary subsidies and other taxes. Immigration from the countryside helped but it did not make up for the loss of population. Some towns and cities also suffered from a decline in trade. The decline was by no means universal though. For example: Coventry prospered until the 1460s; York flourished in the later fourteenth century; and Norwich doubled in population and increased in wealth during the fifteenth century. Of the fifteen towns with populations

CREDITON

TIVERTON
(RIVER EXE)

HADLEIGH
(RIVER BLETT)
WOOL TOWN

BECCLES
(RIVER WAVENEY)

between 2,000 and 3,000 in 1524, four (Crediton and Tiverton in Devon, Hadleigh in Essex and Beccles in Suffolk) had risen from nowhere. If there is a pattern to be detected, it appears to be that towns and cities now prospered in the home counties and in certain textile areas where most of the country's wealth now lay. Changes in trade also affected urban centres either adversely or favourably.

The fortunes of Bristol, Coventry and Norwich benefited from the booming cloth trade but some other centres, such as York, suffered from competition from smaller cloth manufacturing towns, such as Halifax, Leeds and Wakefield. Even Bristol and Norwich were entering a recession by the early sixteenth century. The decline in the export of wool hit established major ports such as Boston and Hull and places such as Lincoln which had held famous wool fairs.

In towns, the hierarchy characteristic of rural England broke down. Towns and cities were governed by narrow civic elites (largely composed of merchants and wealthy leading craftsmen) and served by groups of salaried civil servants. The social and economic life of the towns was dominated by the craft gilds. The rules and regulations of the gilds had to be approved by the town or city government. The gilds regulated wages, hours and conditions of work, the training of craftsmen and the quality and price of goods. They appear to have played an important role in limiting discontent through regulation and arbitration. These craft gilds are not to be confused with religious gilds or fraternities (brotherhoods), which sometimes overlapped with and reinforced the wealthy crafts gilds (as the Corpus Christi gild at Coventry did[11]) but in other cases brought together groups of much humbler people (as was the case with the Corpus Christi gild at Lincoln). The city governors were themselves members of the craft gilds. To see the towns and cities and their populations as entirely separate from the rest of England would, however, be a mistake. Many gentry had houses and interests in both town and country, for example, and connections with men of trade and finance.

---

[11] Corpus Christi means 'body of Christ'.

Summary

The changes in the fabric of English society have relevance for two of our themes. In retrospect, we can see that feudal society was changing and that the authority of the king was being strengthened as a result. We can also see that producers and consumers were being affected in many ways. The Black Death had profound and long-lasting social and economic implications – for example, in the area of labour relations and wages. Although the feudal system still persisted in some respects, the extent to which labour was tied to particular land and lordships was reduced. The growth of particular towns and specific trades should also be noted. Occupations such as the pawnbroker (Figure 3.7) and the moneychanger assumed new importance. Towns developed to serve the needs of their hinterlands but they also developed in response to the consumer demands of their own populations. These socio-economic changes also had political reverberations, as townspeople threw off their obligations to the nobility, asserted their right to govern themselves with crown permission, and acknowledged the lordship only of the king.

Figure 3.7   Occupations such as pawnbroking developed with the growth of towns and trade. The Pawnbroker, in *Tractatum de Septem Vitiis*, late fourteenth century. British Library, Add 27695 f. 7 v. Photo: The Bridgeman Art Library, London

THE WARS OF THE ROSES

Now it is time to turn to what have come to be known after the event as the Wars of the Roses. Were they symptomatic of existing weaknesses in that state? How far did they tear apart the English state?

Context

There were several phases in the Wars of the Roses. The conflict began as the political struggle between Edmund Beaufort, duke of Somerset, and Richard, duke of York (the greatest landowner in England after the king), and eventually drew into its orbit other struggles among the aristocracy. But for his illegitimate descent, Edmund would have been Henry VI's male heir in 1450. Although he had been in command in France during the severe losses of 1449 and 1450, he returned to England unaffected by defeat. Queen Margaret of Anjou and many of the royal household turned to him as their protector. Richard of York was the closest in the legitimate line of succession in 1450. He was full of resentment about his treatment by the crown (especially about being made Lieutenant of Ireland and thus exiled from court). He feared that Somerset would use his influence with Henry VI to have the statute that barred the Beauforts from the succession overturned. Over the next few years, government disintegrated and a fierce civil war broke out.

EXERCISE

Turn now to the account of the Wars of the Roses in the reading by Maurice Keen, *England in the Later Middle Ages*, in the secondary sources. Read this account for a narrative of the Wars of the Roses. You should use the chronology in the *Course Guide* in conjunction with this account. Make brief notes as an *aide memoire*.

Spend no more than about 90 minutes on this exercise.

Causes

Malcolm Vale and other historians suggest that, after the loss of the French territories, we see the working out at home of the consequences of losing French possessions and power. Genealogy, however, undoubtedly provides one of the keys to the conflict that occurred during these years and which has gripped the popular imagination ever since – the Wars of the Roses. During the fourteenth and fifteenth centuries there were no fewer than seven depositions (removal of the king), of which five occurred in the period 1461–85.

Historians search for the causes of change in the past. Causes can be divided into those that are immediate and those that are underlying and often much deeper. Traditionally historians have seen the root causes of the Wars of the Roses as a long-term decline in the strength of the monarchy. It could be, however, that the wars were attributable to much more immediate circumstances that had little bearing on the weakness of the monarchy as an institution.

By looking closely at the family tree of Edward III (reigned 1327–77) you can establish for yourself some of the principal and immediate 'causes' of the Wars of the Roses.

Examine the simplified family tree of the extended family of Edward III (*Visual Sources*, Plate 3.1). Spend a few minutes examining it carefully. In what ways were the Wars of the Roses the result of a family squabble over the crown of England? Write your answer in note form.

Spend about 15 minutes on this exercise.

- All the claimants to the English throne during the fifteenth century traced their claim to Edward III.

- Edward's descendants intermarried at various points (e.g. Cicely Neville, descendant of House of Lancaster, married Richard duke of York and was the mother of Edward IV and Richard III of the House of York; and Elizabeth of York, daughter of Edward IV, became Henry VII of Lancaster's wife).

- Only the marriage of Elizabeth of York to Henry Tudor (earl of Richmond) successfully reconciled the two houses in the crown.

- Several possible claimants to the throne died in, or as a direct result of, battles of the Hundred Years War and the Wars of the Roses (e.g. Edward, Prince of Wales, son of Henry VI, died at the battle of Tewkesbury in 1471; Edmund Beaufort, duke of Somerset, was killed at the battle of St Albans in 1455, his eldest son Henry was executed at Hexham in 1464 and two of his sons were killed at Tewkesbury in 1471; Warwick the Kingmaker was killed in the same year at the Battle of Barnet; Richard, duke of York, died at the battle of Wakefield in 1460 and, of course, his son Richard III (Edward IV's brother) was killed at Bosworth Field

- The failure of the male line, either through early death or through all-female descent, was evident (e.g. John Beaufort, duke of Somerset, was succeeded by a daughter, Margaret, who married into the House of Tudor; Richard, earl of Warwick, had heiresses, Anne and Isobel; Henry VI's son Edward died in the same year that his father was murdered; Edward, Prince of Wales, son of Richard of Gloucester and Anne Neville, predeceased his father in 1484 – this ignores the most famous early deaths of Edward V and Richard, duke of York, who were presumed murdered in 1483, shortly after the death of their father Edward IV).

Interpretations

The problems of the succession, however, combined with other circumstances to aggravate the situation. If you read a book on the Wars of the Roses published before the 1980s, you will probably come across interpretations that differ markedly from those written since. *Past* historians have suggested that the most obvious causes of the conflict were the following.

- On the death of Henry V at such a young age, the monarchy and the Lancaster line were weakened by the accession of a minor, Henry VI, who was mentally ill for much of his reign. (There are distinct parallels here with the ways in which the civil wars in France in the earlier fifteenth century developed out of competition for influence at the court of a king who was insane for much of the time.)

- The bankruptcy of the crown by mismanagement exposed Henry VI's position yet more – this dated from Edward III's reign, when Edward had made concessions in order to finance his wars against France.

- The Lancastrians were also potentially weakened by their association with defeat in France; York appealed to those who had suffered from the loss of Normandy and Guyenne.

- The emergence of another line descended from Edward III through his fifth son, Edmund of Langley, and especially his ambitious grandson Richard, duke of York.

- There was no generally accepted set of rules governing the succession to the throne or the circumstances in which a deficient monarch might be deposed and replaced. Male primogeniture (i.e. the first-born male descendant will succeed) was the norm, but what if the king was bad or mad? In those circumstances might the king be deposed (even killed) and his place filled with a claimant who was female or even of illegitimate descent (like the Beaufort/Neville and the Beaufort/Tudor lines)? Edward III had allowed this situation to develop because he gave his surviving younger sons important estates and titles. This gave them wealth, status and patronage, which allowed them to set themselves and their houses up as rivals to the monarchs. This was not just something which became important in 1460.

- The willingness of prominent nobles (often of royal descent) to exploit the situation to their own advantage, and to bring in their retainers and supporters to the conflict, promoted and extended the conflict and broadened its impact. They were ignorant illiterates who behaved like barbarians and, in marked contrast to the gentry, thought only of their own betterment. Edward III had encouraged them to build up their power and influence. When the nobles left France, they returned to wreak havoc in England.

SPECIMEN ANSWER

Turn now to Anthology Document 1.22 and read the extracts from Sir John Fortescue's *Governance of England* on the shortcomings of Henry VI's governance of England.

What principal evils does Fortescue identify? Answer in brief note form.

Spend about 30 minutes on this exercise.

SPECIMEN ANSWER

- The crown was financially bankrupt.
- The council did not include sufficient wise and selfless individuals who had the good of the kingdom or 'commonweal' at heart.
- Nobles and their retainers had too much power and influence.

DISCUSSION

Were you startled by the style in which Fortescue wrote? There is relatively little reference to specifics and a good deal of generalisation. When Fortescue names individuals, these are figures from history; references to contemporaries such as the earl of Warwick are oblique.

Refer back to Fortescue, chapter 9, and you will see that he comments on the relationship between the monarch's authority or sovereignty on the one hand, and his power and wealth on the other. At the time when he is writing, an individual king's authority is unassailable only as long as he maintains his power over all his subjects; if a subject attains equal power, he challenges the king's position and threatens to overthrow him. Once this seems possible, the king's subjects will be tempted to follow the challenger.

Fortescue argues that certain institutional changes will protect the king against these evils or even remove them altogether. His is a prescription for change.

You could well conclude that past historians relied heavily on Fortescue's diagnosis of England's problems. Keen suggests that contemporaries, both Lancastrian and Yorkist, appear to have agreed with him, even though they did not necessarily agree with his proposed remedies (Keen, 1973, pp. 394–411).

The importance of legal arguments regarding the succession is a subject for debate. It is true that Sir John Fortescue (a Lancastrian supporter – he was Henry VI's chief justice) and Yorkist propagandists laid great emphasis on the legality or illegality of the claims to the throne lodged by individuals such as Henry VI, Richard of York and Edward, earl of March (later Edward IV).

Fortescue and the claims of Richard of York to the throne

Fortescue argued that 'by the laws of God and of nature' a woman could not succeed to the throne or pass on the right to it. He also suggested that Philippa, daughter of Lionel of Clarence, was illegitimate.

It is worth looking back to the family tree of Edward III (*Visual Sources*, Plate 3.1) to see how this theory undermined York's claim and that of Edward IV and his brothers. It also affected the eventual claim of Henry VII (Tudor) to the throne. He was descended from Edward III's son, John of Gaunt, through Gaunt's illegitimate progeny and through his own mother, Margaret Beaufort. Henry considered it extremely important to strengthen his claim to the throne but found that he had to do so through the weak (because she was female) claim of his wife, Elizabeth, eldest daughter of the Yorkist king, Edward IV.

Fortescue, sent into a long exile because of his support for Henry VI and the Lancastrians, certainly robustly defended Henry VI's right to the throne against the Yorkists. Yorkists, on the other hand, condemned the Lancastrian regime as a usurpation of the legal succession. All the ills that had befallen England and its kings were the result of the deposition of Richard II in 1399 – Henry IV had had leprosy; Henry V had died young; Henry VI was mad. Modern historians seek to place this emphasis on the legal issue in context. Yes, the issue of inheritance was important, but probably not as important as possession of the crown and ability to hold on to it.

> A few families, bound by interest or loyalty to the House of Lancaster, proved irreconcilable to a Yorkist regime: the heirs of Somerset, the earls of Oxford and the Tudors. But even among the

peers the majority could usually be relied upon to rally to the king *de facto,* if he could hold his own, without too much regard to his title *de jure*.

(Keen, 1973, p. 462)

K.B. Macfarlane (1973) showed how this affected Henry VI's kingship. He suggested that Henry VI failed in good lordship – he did not build up a body of noble retainers who owed loyalty to him alone. This was partly – perhaps largely – because of his mental incapacity. Other patrons held the loyalty of his subjects. The king's illness had divided the aristocracy into those who profited from his continuance on the throne and those who did not. Those who objected had no alternative to taking up arms against the king. Others argued that the outbreak of war can be explained almost entirely in terms of aristocratic rivalries and the social disorder that resulted from bastard feudalism.

The implications of the personalities and the personal attributes of key participants must not be underestimated either. For example, the conflict might have been brought to a conclusion after the position of Henry VI was successfully defended by his indomitable queen, Margaret of Anjou, who rallied the Lancastrian troops after York's victory at the Battle of St Albans in 1455 and the decisive Lancastrian victory at Ludford in 1459. (See Figure 3.8 for an illustration of the piety of St Henry VI, which helped his queen rally support.) However, the Lancastrians alienated the defeated Yorkists and their heirs yet more by seizing their estates, and Richard of York returned from exile to fight again and win a major victory at Northampton in the summer of 1460. Richard was not very astute and he failed to make political capital out of this victory when he came to London. He also left his troops open to attack as he left his Yorkshire stronghold in Wakefield in December 1460. Conversely, Edward IV's political acumen enabled him to establish strong government and effectively bring the wars to an end for two long periods.

More recent interpretations

It is important to note some points that are highly relevant when we consider the strength of the English state at this time. Currently historians disagree with some aspects of this analysis of the causes of the Wars of the Roses. First, while the accession and rule of Henry VI did put an unbearable strain eventually on the Lancastrian hold on the crown, the underlying strength of that institution meant that Henry VI *was* able to hold on successfully for some years before his first deposition and that monarchical rule continued relatively undisturbed during that period. It is argued that the crown was not financially bankrupt either. Second, when Edward IV became king (see Figure 3.9), especially after the final deposition of Henry VI in 1470, he built up the role of the royal household in government. (At one time it was fashionable to see this as part of a movement towards new monarchies in Europe.) Modern historians now believe that the old view that the Wars of the Roses were symptomatic of (and largely caused by) a long-term decline in the strength of the English monarchy is incorrect (Carpenter, 1997, p. 19).

Figure 3.8   Henry VI's reputation as a saint helped his queen to rally support. St Henry VI, left, and St Edmund from the south aisle chapel screen, St Michael's Church, Barton Turf, Norfolk. Photo: © National Monuments Record / H. Felton 13317 AA49/5943

Figure 3.9   Contemporary paintings of early kings are few. This familiar portrait of Edward IV dates from the mid sixteenth century but was probably based on an earlier image, unknown artist, *c* 1540, oil on panel, 33 x 27 cm. © National Portrait Gallery, London, NPG 3642

What, in any event, is meant by strength? If we mean that the monarch did not exercise a centralised, interventionist rule over all parts of the kingdom, enforcing the rule of law, then it is true that he did not. However, no one at the time, and certainly not the king and his noble subjects, conceived of government or the state in that way. They did not find Henry VI lacking in this respect, but they did find him lacking in others, such as his inability to choose wise counsellors. (In order to understand the situation we need to divest ourselves of modern ideas of what strong central government should do.)

Earlier interpretations that saw the deposition of Henry VI as a stage in the development of a constitutional monarchy, and which emphasised the appeals that Richard of York made to parliament as a body representative of the will of the people, have also been dismissed.

In fact, in 'normal' circumstances the late medieval English constitution could work quite well and the state was not unravelling. The problem was that the circumstances in mid- to late-fifteenth-century England were far from normal and the constitution was therefore subject to abnormal stresses and strains. A leading modern authority on the Wars of the Roses, Christine Carpenter, believes that there were no long-term constitutional weaknesses bringing about conflict. Neither, in her view, did the main conflict arise out of escalating local feuds between nobles. The conflict arose out of a specific problem: the king (Henry VI) was insane and incapable and there were ambitious, rival claimants – 'It was the failure of kingship ... which caused both the feuding and the battles ... It was the failure of central governance that led to local conflict and ultimately made conflict among the nobles nationally divisive' (Carpenter, 1997, p. 253). It is worth noting that Richard of York (like the duke of Burgundy) always claimed that he was fighting for the cause of better government and purging the court and council, and appealed for popular support through propaganda. Note the crucial distinction drawn here between the institution of monarchy ('the crown') and the person of the king ('kingship'). 'What there was from about 1437 was quite simply a crisis of kingship which threatened eventually to become a crisis of the crown' (Carpenter, 1997, p. 255).

How far do suggestions that lack of success in France and a desire among the Yorkists to regain French lands also contributed to the downfall of the House of Lancaster bear close scrutiny? Remember what Malcolm Vale said about this in the secondary source 'The end and aftermath of the hundred years war'. It is true that Richard of York had served in France and focused later upon Somerset's loss of Normandy as a cause of conflict, but in fact few of his supporters had any stake in France and few supporters on either side had experience of fighting in the campaigns of the Hundred Years War. From 1437 to 1450, as long as there was hope of regaining lands in France, the nobility stood solidly behind the king. Even when Warwick brought over the Calais garrison in 1459, it made quite clear the strength of its allegiance to the king. Yet it could well be that, as Keen suggested, the psychological blow dealt to national pride, and the real blow dealt to trade, enabled Richard of York to make very effective propaganda against the House of Lancaster. 'The defeat was an important factor in the struggles. It did more than anything else to discredit the court party. It gave York ... his opportunity.' It allowed him to appeal to the people on the grounds that 'the common weal of the kingdom had been damaged by the misgovernment of the King's friends' (Keen, 1973, pp. 454–6.)

Neither is it necessary to paint the protagonists as merely greedy and ambitious for power. The situation was impossible. The constitution did not allow for the legitimate existence of an opposition. Power and authority rested with the monarch, who ruled with the advice of councillors chosen by him. When a king behaved deplorably, the 'political nation' (i.e. those whose views counted) united behind a deposition. In the case of Henry VI, the king was mad, not bad; therefore, the political nation did not speak with one voice to depose him when his incompetence became glaringly obvious on his reaching adult years. Ultimately this led to armed conflict when two men put themselves forward as potential regents in 1450 – the duke of York and the duke of Somerset.

Summary

Interpretations of the causes and course of the Wars of the Roses vary. Nineteenth- and earlier twentieth-century interpretations tended to emphasise the weakness of the Lancastrian monarchy and the Wars of the Roses as a symptom. The development of a constitutional monarchy was stressed. More recent interpretations suggest that the crisis was one of an individual (Henry VI) and not of the institution of monarchy itself. Some point to the absence of any legitimate means of expressing peaceful opposition as the key to the outbreak of armed hostilities. They also downplay the significance of the wars themselves.

Terminology: were the Wars of the Roses really wars?

Is it appropriate to call the Wars of the Roses 'wars' at all? What effect did they have on the people of England? These linked questions have a bearing both on the theme of the formation of the state and on that of producers and consumers.

If you look back at the chronology of events in the *Course Guide*, you will see that over the period 1422–89 there were, in fact, very few major battles, especially battles for control of or possession of the crown. Some of the battles, for example those at Heworth and at Nibley Green, were extensions of private and local feuds, and these are not included in the chronology. 'It is understood that armies were mostly not large and campaigns were short and that the potential for large scale destruction between 1455 and 1485 was much less than has been supposed' (Carpenter, 1997, p. 21). Armies were not kept long in the field because this was too expensive. Historians still debate how much damage was caused, but certainly there was no wholesale destruction. Sieges were few and therefore pillaging, whereby the attacking armies fed themselves, was largely absent. In 1461 Margaret of Anjou's army stayed in the field after the Battle of Wakefield (December 1460). Its plunder of the countryside was commented on because it was so unusual. There were also quite a few extended periods of peace, especially during the second reign of Edward IV (1471–83). Indeed, most historians now agree that the Wars of the Roses really ended in 1471 and were recommenced briefly and by accident in 1483.

Yet we must be wary of writing the Wars of the Roses off as a 'brief and harmless episode' because historians have done relatively little work on their repercussions. It does seem that the lower orders, the 'commons', advanced in political awareness as a result of the wars. This may have been of more importance than any direct social and economic effects on them. Economically, the church, a major landholder, was little affected by the conflict because its lands were immune. Most profoundly affected in economic, social and political terms were the lay or secular landowners, especially the nobility. Carpenter argues that they tried for the most part to stay neutral, but that this was out of an instinct for survival not lack of interest (Carpenter, 1997, p. 261). The old view that the nobility was effectively wiped out by the Wars of the Roses, thus clearing the way for the so-called Tudor despotism, is now dismissed, but the deaths that did occur probably had an unsettling and demoralising effect.

Certainly the royal houses of England, and those of some of the nobility, suffered many fatalities as a result of the Wars of the Roses. Four members of the important Courtenay family in the direct male line died between 1461 and 1471. However, historians suggest that noble and royal losses were not, in general, matched by the rest of the population. There was, of course, some disruption of families, and historians identify occasions when the Wars of the Roses had an impact on the lives of young wives. For example, Margery Etchingham married William Blount, Lord Mountjoy, who was killed at Barnet on 14 April 1471. She was in the market for a second husband for a while and eventually she remarried. But, in fact, it is remarkable how many families managed to avoid any involvement in the wars. For example, the Stonors of Oxfordshire, despite kinship with Edmund Hampden (who was at court and suffered exile and then death at Tewkesbury on the side of Henry VI), managed to escape relatively unscathed and not really committed to one side or the other until the battle of Stoke, when much of the Midlands turned out.

THE STATE AND STATE FORMATION: THE STRUGGLE FOR THE CROWN AND THE INVOLVEMENT OF THE GENTRY AND THE NOBILITY

It is important to set all this in the context of our study of state formation. Late-fifteenth-century England was not rebelling against the institution of monarchy or, indeed, the role of the aristocracy. Rather, it was engaged in a struggle to determine who should be king and who among the nobility should hold sway. Relatively few people were involved in this struggle and the few real battles that occurred did not result in wholesale destruction of the kingdom or its population. The war was not fought to query the monarch's sovereignty or to further the role of the parliament in state government. Nevertheless, there is a suggestion that the political awareness of the groups below the nobility was heightened during this period.

Sources historians use to study the period of the Wars of the Roses

Historians use a great variety of types of source. These include official records, personal correspondence, estate documents, accounts, legal documents and wills. It is important to note that interpretations will depend on which sources were employed. (It has been suggested that the old derogatory view of the nobility as exploitative and barbaric derives from the fact that no large cache of noble letters and papers survives.)

One of the first actions you should take when reading a modern historical work is to check what sources were employed – look at the footnotes and the references or bibliography carefully. The next piece of work shows why this is important in the context of the Wars of the Roses. First of all, let us acquaint ourselves more fully with two gentry families from the shires that you have met already – the Pastons of East Anglia and the Stonors from the Midlands – who were locally important landowners below the ranks of the nobility.

The gentry

The Pastons

If you have heard of any fifteenth century individuals other than those named in the history plays of Shakespeare, then you have probably encountered the Pastons of Norfolk, who took their name from the village twenty miles from Norwich in which they lived. They are well known because their voluminous correspondence has survived and because modern editions of this correspondence have been printed. There is no doubt that the Paston letters are a major source for English society below the nobility during the period from about 1420 until the early sixteenth century. How typical the family was is, however, another issue, as is the extent to which it was usual for families below the nobility to engage in such extensive written communication. The story of the family is certainly somewhat confusing, largely because a very limited number of first names were used! Don't worry too much about this as no one will be expecting you to remember all this detail.

> **The Pastons**
>
> **Clement Paston** (*c*.1355–1388) was a small landowner in fourteenth-century Norfolk who borrowed money to send his sons to school. His investment bore rich dividends, for his son **William Paston I** (1378–1444) rose from these relatively humble beginnings to be a lawyer and a judge. The sons of William and his wife **Agnes**, who were born between 1421 and 1442, built on this tradition by attending either or both Cambridge University and the London Inns of Court. **William Paston II** (1436–1496) even married into the nobility when he wed **Lady Anne Beaufort**, daughter of **Edmund, duke of Somerset**, who belonged to the illegitimate royal line. A later generation, the children of **John Paston I** (1421–1466), who were born in the 1460s, to some extent broke the tradition of using university and legal education as the foundation of their

fortunes and instead made their way through service in royal and noble households.

The Pastons present a relatively good example of a family which, at times, certainly profited from serving the nobility, but which also suffered when it came into conflict with the same. William Paston I rose in the service of the dukes of Norfolk, eventually becoming the duke's steward in 1415. He went on to become a justice of the peace and eventually sergeant-at-law and judge of the Court of Common Pleas. His sons John Paston I and William Paston II both became Norfolk JPs and William II also became a member of parliament. John I, through his marriage with **Margaret Mautby**, of Mautby near Yarmouth, came to know her relative **Sir John Fastolf**, who had won great estates and wealth during the Hundred Years War. (Fastolf was the basis of Shakespeare's character Falstaff in the play *Henry IV*.) John I became one of Fastolf's executors and heir to Caister Castle and other properties on Fastolf's death in 1459. John I spent the remainder of his life defending his claim to Caister and other properties. (In 1465, the duke of Suffolk sent armed retainers to attack his manor of Hellesdon, near Norwich.) His successor **John Paston II** (1442–1479) tried to settle the issue of possession of the Fastolf inheritance, but he was temporarily thwarted when the duke of Norfolk's men laid siege to Caister. It was Norfolk's death in 1476 that confirmed John II in possession. **John Paston III** (1444–1504) (rather confusingly called John despite being the younger brother, by two years, of John II) became part of the duke of Norfolk's retinue in the 1460s.

The importance of the Pastons was largely local, although John I, his brother William II and John's two eldest sons (John II and John III) did serve for periods in parliament. How did the Wars of the Roses have an impact on the lives of the Pastons? John II joined the household of the young King Edward IV when he seized the throne for the first time in 1461. His brother John III fought with the duke of Norfolk's retainers on behalf of the Yorkists in the 1460s. These two brothers formed part of the retinue of Margaret of York when she went to Bruges to marry the duke of Burgundy in 1468. By 1471, however, they had worn the emblem of the restored Lancastrian Henry VI at the Battle of Barnet. It has been suggested that their broken allegiance was a response to the duke of Norfolk's own failure of good lordship in his attacks on Paston claims to Caister Castle. Once they had been granted pardons by the restored Edward IV they again served the Yorkist cause.

EXERCISE

You are now going to use the Paston correspondence as a source for the Wars of the Roses. Turn to Anthology Document 1.24 (e) and (f). Read these extracts carefully and write brief notes for each letter separately under the following headings:

- What is this document?
- Who wrote it?
- When was it written?
- Who was it sent to?
- Why was it written?

How useful are these short letters to historians in their study of the Wars of the Roses? What, in particular, do they contribute to our knowledge of the impact of the wars on the population? (Remember to consult your chronology in the *Course Guide*, the text of this unit and the reading by Maurice Keen, *England in the Later Middle Ages*, in the secondary sources, to help you with the context here.)

Spend about 45 minutes on this exercise.

SPECIMEN ANSWER

These are short but complicated letters written by her two eldest sons (John II and John III) to Margaret Paston. In each case, the writer alludes to many individuals and places, and the historian has to try to identify these in order to make good use of the evidence. The first letter is useful because it shows how the Paston family hoped to benefit from the good lordship of the earl of Oxford (a Lancastrian) and the duke of Norfolk (a Yorkist) through John III's services. Despite the fact that John III and John II had recently supported the Yorkist cause, they thus hoped to benefit from the restoration of Henry VI. The letter may be used to establish what was happening in this period shortly after Henry VI's restoration (Warwick had landed in Kent in September, Edward IV fled the kingdom on 2 October and Henry VI was to be (re)crowned on the following day, 13 October 1470), the rumours that were flying around and the expectations that were raised. The second letter gives some account of the battle of Barnet four days earlier, of John III's injury during that battle, of the deaths of important players on both sides (such as the earl of Warwick) and of other events consequent on the battle (such as the imprisonment of the archbishop). It also gives the writer's view of the situation. Although the brothers had fought on the losing Lancastrian side at the Battle of Barnet, their previous allegiance had been Yorkist and one might (in the light of such knowledge) detect some satisfaction in John II's prediction that Edward IV will soon drive Margaret of Anjou from the country once again. Both letters suggest to historians how important private correspondence was at this time as a means of communicating national and local news, and they confirm that such news was regarded as important by gentlemen in the countryside.

DISCUSSION

These letters do have their defects as sources, however. The 'accounts' are far from detailed and they need to be verified. You will have seen from the notes that none of the men that John III thought would be executed on 12 October met that fate, for instance.

Personal papers present a particular 'take' on historical events and situations. Historians need to compare this 'take' with the versions offered in other sources, selecting these from as wide a variety of types of source as possible. Where accounts differ, the historian has to weigh up the relative 'authority' of the sources as well as the possible biases they contain.

The Stonors

The Stonor family, who lived in Stonor on the Buckinghamshire/Oxfordshire border, is another gentry family for which extensive papers survive. Historians have concluded that the Stonors were more representative in many ways of the English gentry than were the Pastons, and it is for this reason that attention is given them here. The Stonors, in common with many contemporaries, rose in society through the profits of the legal profession. By the late fourteenth century, they were playing a leading role in local politics and society. Christine Carpenter has reconstructed their 'circle' or 'connection' (see box).

The Stonors

Thomas Stonor I who had close links to **Thomas Chaucer** and through him to the royal administration and perhaps even to **Henry Beaufort**, Chaucer's patron, increased his local influence. He strengthened his position by marrying the heir to the bishop of Salisbury. The Chaucer connection seems also to have led **Thomas Stonor II** into the circle of **William de la Pole**, duke of Suffolk. Suffolk was married to Thomas Chaucer's heiress. Thomas Stonor II probably married an illegitimate daughter of Suffolk. He served on the Oxfordshire Commission of the Peace from 1466 alongside the duke of Suffolk. Thomas Stonor II held on to this position until his death in 1474. (Carpenter, 1995.)

The Stonors were *survivors* because they avoided over-commitment to either side during the Wars of the Roses. Thomas Stonor II was a member of parliament for Oxfordshire in 1447 and 1449, and sheriff of Oxfordshire and Berkshire in 1453. He served on both anti-Yorkist (1459, 1460) and Yorkist (1462) commissions of array. He did not become embroiled in the wars. Among his connections, only **Edmund Hampden**, closely linked with the court, and **Peter Marmion** strongly supported the Lancastrian cause and suffered the penalty – Hampden died at the battle of Tewkesbury and Marmion was forced to give up his manor of Nursling after that battle. (Carpenter, 1996, pp. 5–6.)

Thomas's heir, **William Stonor**, used the ensuing period to build up his local influence and continued to keep his head well below the parapet nationally. Only once, in 1483, did William misjudge the situation by openly joining a rebellion against Richard III. Like so many English gentry over the fourteenth and fifteenth centuries, the Stonors performed little military service: during the Wars of the Roses they probably fought only at the battle of Stoke, which was notable for drawing many Midland families into the fray. Unlike the Pastons, whose enlargement of their land holdings severely aggravated their neighbours, the Stonor family built up their landed estates without alienating their neighbours.

Summary

Contemporary letters can help us to determine the extent to which later-fifteenth-century England was war-torn and violent, and the extent to which it was dominated by noble influence. However, correspondence has limitations as a source. For the most part historians are presented with a one-sided conversation. The reader has to deduce the immediate context of the letter writing – the writer's mood and motivation and relationship with the recipient. The account of events contained in letters can be partial, personal and prejudiced.

The Paston letters show a family who were caught up in national events and who seem to illustrate well the impact of 'bastard feudalism'. If historians used only this one collection they would be justified in concluding that fifteenth-century society was violent and that the gentry were involved in the Wars of the Roses as a result of their relationship of service to the nobility and the crown. The Stonor letters, however, show a different, much gentler society. Because this collection deals with the humdrum lives of the Stonors as well as with their political, military and social engagement or non-engagement, it provides a more balanced view of gentry life during the wars. As a result of reading both collections together, historians may be led to show fifteenth-century gentry life in all its complexity. The sources lend credence to the view that allegiances during this period were astonishingly fluid. The importance of 'bastard feudalism' or 'lordship' in the social, political and military areas cannot be discounted, but it must be acknowledged that, for many of the gentry, this was not a period dominated by conflict and agitation, by involvement in national affairs as a result of bastard feudal relations, but rather one in which they sought to consolidate their local positions and to live lives as far as possible untouched by the wars.

We can use the examples of the Stonor and Paston families to make an important point about the extent to which the nobility dominated fifteenth-century English society and politics. The Pastons lived in Norfolk, where the rule of the dukes of Norfolk was very evident; the Stonors, on the other hand, came from a part of England where noble domination was less evident, probably because the crown was the chief landowner.

The nobility

A glance back at the chronology in the *Course Guide* and at the family tree of Edward III's descendants (*Visual Sources*, Plate 3.1) suggests that the relationship of bastard feudalism (lordship) between the claimants to the monarchy and the nobility was crucially important. The aspirations of the nobles and the ways in which the king acted as their good lord, their patron, are central to the story. Sometimes the Wars of the Roses are shown as a struggle in which the claimants to the throne are successful to the extent that they can *buy* the support of the strongest nobles.

Nevilles, Beauchamps, Woodvilles

One of the most prominent members of the nobility involved in the Wars of the Roses was Richard Neville (1428–1471), earl of Warwick and Salisbury. He succeeded his father Richard as earl of Salisbury in 1460, but his claim to the title of earl of Warwick came through his marriage in 1449 to Anne, sole heiress to Richard de Beauchamp, earl of Warwick (1382–1439), when her brother Henry de Beauchamp, duke of Warwick, died without an heir in 1445.

EXERCISE

Look back now at the chronology in the *Course Guide* and at your notes on the chapters about the Wars of the Roses in the reading by Maurice Keen, *England in the*

Later Middle Ages, in the secondary sources, and note Richard Neville's part in events.

Spend about 15 minutes on this exercise.

Warwick began as a staunch supporter of the Yorkist cause of Richard, duke of York, and his heir Edward, earl of March, but switched sides in the later 1460s, eventually declaring for the cause of Henry VI of Lancaster in 1470.

Later commentators dubbed Warwick 'the Kingmaker' and certainly he played his part in promoting first the Yorkist and then the Lancastrian cause. (His change of sides was the result of Warwick's eclipse at court by the Woodville family and his awareness of Edward IV's own independence of mind.) This is a good example of the way in which a prominent nobleman could affect the fortunes of the monarchy. For our purposes, however, it is more important to determine how powerful Warwick was, how he achieved this position and to what extent he had a lasting effect on the English state.

The rise and fall of Warwick

First note the way that marriage was used to strengthen Warwick. He was of royal blood himself – his grandmother had been Joan Beaufort, illegitimate daughter of John of Gaunt, fourth son of Edward III, and Katherine Swynford. Joan had made a good marriage to Ralph Neville, earl of Westmoreland. Turn to the images from the Beauchamp Pageant Book, which are provided on the course website with the secondary sources. Two of these images are also available in *Visual Sources,* Plates 3.4 and 3.5. Here we see how keen Warwick's wife Anne Beauchamp was to demonstrate her own descent. Indeed, she commissioned the beautifully illustrated account of her father Richard Beauchamp, earl of Warwick, to that very end. Richard Neville's claim to the throne was, however, weak and he sought power through influence over the monarch. If you look at Edward III's family tree (*Visual Sources*, Plate 3.1) you will note that Richard Neville earl of Salisbury's sister Cicely had married Richard, duke of York, thus cementing a Yorkist connection. She was aunt to Warwick the Kingmaker. It was the Yorkist cause that Warwick the Kingmaker sought to promote with his personal support and that of his own followers. In addition, he negotiated marriage alliances for his heiresses that were designed to ensure that his own heirs eventually sat close to the throne. Anne, his younger daughter, was first married to the heir of Henry VI and Margaret of Anjou, but when Edward, Prince of Wales, died in 1471 she was married to Richard, duke of Gloucester. His elder daughter Isabel was married to George, duke of Clarence. They were sisters-in-law to the king and aunts to his children; their own children would be first cousins to the future king. In the Beauchamp Pageant Book the importance of Warwick's dynasty and the links between his lineage and that of the crown are stressed (see the course website).

Warwick also had enormous landed interests in many parts of the kingdom. With his lands came influence – this was particularly true in the north. For example, the Redesdale Rebellion in Yorkshire in 1469 against Edward IV seems to have been led by nobles, kinsmen and tenants of Warwick. The leader was probably of the Conyers family, a kinsman of the earl by marriage and his steward at Middleham, Yorkshire, centre of the earl's northern lands. Three of the minor nobility involved – Fitzhugh, Latimer and Dudley – belonged to the Warwick connection. Many other participants were tenants of the earl. This seems to be an excellent example of the way in which bastard feudalism operated. (See Anthology Document 1.23 for indentures of life service.)

It must not be supposed, however, that the relationships described as bastard feudalism were simple or that the earl of Warwick was able to command the loyalty of all the knights, squires, gentry and tenants in a given locality. Carpenter's study of Warwickshire society has demonstrated that, within that county, local nobility such as the duke of Norfolk, the Ferrers of Chartley and the duke of Buckingham had substantial landholdings and networks of influence. In that county Richard Neville, earl of Warwick, also suffered in the 1450s from being a newcomer to its networks – the Beauchamp earls of Warwick (see DVD 1, The Beauchamp Chapel, Warwick) had had a natural alliance with lesser landowners, but Richard Neville, a northerner with no knowledge of Midland politics, found that using this alliance to its full advantage was by no means automatic or easy (Carpenter, 1992, p. 448). It was not until the early 1460s, during the minority of Buckingham's heir, that Warwick found himself to be all-powerful in Warwickshire. His position was no longer challenged to the south and west of Warwick by landholders such as Sudeley and Beauchamp of Powick, who had formerly been in favour at court but were now rejected by Edward IV (Carpenter, 1992, p. 489). Unfortunately for Warwick, it was not long before alternative networks re-emerged in north and north-east Warwickshire under the leadership of Sudeley and William Lord Hastings. Yet in the first half of the 1460s, all the known MPs, most of the justices of the peace and all of the sheriffs were men in the earl of Warwick's service.

Nevertheless, it was another matter to convert this dominance into making the county landholders accept his intervention in local affairs. County life was markedly unsettled during the 1460s in a series of minor and major disputes about land and inheritance. Warwick's local standing was seriously damaged by his failure to assert his good lordship in attacks on Burdet property and against Richard Verney for violence against the earl's clients the Dalbys. He was responsible for creating local tensions himself when, in the 1450s, he imported retainers from northern families to Meriden and Berkswell. These retainers did not assimilate well into local landholding networks and became embroiled in a number of messy court cases, which the earl of Warwick failed to clear up. In the course of the 1460s, this resulted in divisions among the earl's own followers, who supported different sides in the various quarrels. 'There are good grounds for believing that what was really happening was that his affinity was splitting apart and that, if he was trying to limit the damage, he was not being successful' (Carpenter, 1992, p. 501).

The importance of fortuitous genealogical 'events' in the making of a state is again worthy of comment. Buckingham had posed a threat to Warwick's power in Warwickshire and the counties that bordered it. When Buckingham died in 1460, shortly after the death of his adult heir, the dukedom was inherited by his infant grandson. Warwick also took charge of the Latimer estates when George Neville, his uncle, was declared insane. This strengthened Warwick's position by giving him a firm foothold on the Northamptonshire border.

There can be little doubt that Edward IV's deposition in 1470 owed most to Warwick's personal ambition and his ability to command, alongside Clarence, powerful armies, but there were limits to what he could achieve. Warwick could and did take revenge on those he believed to have supplanted him in the king's counsels – Pembroke was executed after the battle of Edgecote, Lord Rivers, the queen's father, and John Woodville, her brother, were executed at Coventry in August. Edward IV was imprisoned in Warwick's own castles, first at Warwick and then at Middleham. After that he could do little. 'The trouble was that Warwick had no authority to rule and dared not attempt any radical restructuring of the political status quo for fear of giving too much offence' (Carpenter, 1992, p. 501).

The Woodvilles had nothing like the power over the king that Warwick alleged. There was little sign that the nobility or the people complained about Edward's rule, for he was regarded as a strong king. (See Figure 3.10, which shows Edward IV and his wife. With them are the causes of future conflict in the kingdom – Edward's minor heir (later Edward V) and Edward IV's younger brother Richard of Gloucester (later Lord Protector and King Richard III. See also *Visual Sources,* Plate 3.2, which shows the Royal Window in Canterbury Cathedral.) Richard of York and Edward had been able to claim that they were removing a king who was totally unfit to rule; Richard of Warwick, on the other hand, could not make such a claim stick. The manifesto of the northern rebels asking for a restoration of good governance, which objected to Edward IV's oppressive taxation, complained of disorder and alleged his alienation of the nobility, bore little scrutiny. If England was in trouble from disorder in 1471, it was largely because of Warwick's own actions in removing Edward. In 1471, the earl of Warwick had to release Edward IV from prison so that the king could suppress a revolt in Henry VI's favour on the northern border and, notably, Edward was able to summon Gloucester, Arundel, Northumberland, Sussex, Essex and Hastings to his side to re-enter London.

Summary

Historians often debate the role played by particular individuals in shaping events and, in this case, the fortunes of the monarchy. Warwick's ambition and his undoubted lordship over men certainly helped him to critical influence in national affairs. Although these were sufficient while England was ruled by an incapable monarch, they proved insufficient when the king was strong and was able to assert good lordship of his own.

Figure 3.10   Edward IV, a strong king, left his throne exposed when he died leaving a minor heir, Edward V. English school, Edward IV with Elizabeth Woodville, Edward V and Richard, Duke of Gloucester, later Richard III, fifteenth century. Lambeth Palace Library, London. Photo: The Bridgeman Art Library, London

DVD exercise

Now turn to DVD 1 and play the section that deals with the Beauchamp Chapel – a monument to Warwick the Kingmaker's predecessor and father-in-law, Richard de Beauchamp. The emphasis here is on the ways in which historians are able to use visual evidence (from architecture, art, artefacts) to understand past societies. The exercises will help you to see how our knowledge of the language of heraldry and genealogy, for example, can help us to understand the 'meaning' of the sources themselves and how this can, in its turn, deepen our understanding of fifteenth-century English society and hierarchical relationships within it.

CONCLUSION

Different interpretations – historiography

Historians, as a matter of course, interest themselves in the history of historical styles/historical interpretations or historiography. In this unit you have been introduced to the views of several historians, past and present. If you read a number of histories of England during the Wars of the Roses written over the last sixty years, you will be struck by the differing interpretations of the same situations and events, the varying styles and fashions. Sometimes you will read that a certain historian's is an 'outdated interpretation' and this perhaps suggests that only very recent works are worth considering. Certainly recent works have the edge on earlier interpretations because they have been able to take advantage of the most recently worked sources and the opinions and insights of later scholars. However, there is often still a place for earlier works, especially those that dealt with subjects no longer fashionable or which were considered so definitive that they could not easily be bettered. The task before you is to disentangle the 'useful' facts from their often outdated and less than useful interpretative framework.

The nature of the state

The loss of the French possessions certainly had an impact on the development of the English state, but in a more complex way than was once thought. It seems unlikely that it contributed significantly to the weakness of Henry VI's position, although it may have alienated some of his potential supporters. It probably strengthened the sense of a specifically English identity and, indirectly, of an independent English state as English attention turned away from France. Nevertheless, it did not lead to isolation from Europe. Rather, it pointed England in a new direction – towards the Low Countries. Burgundy presented a model for the Yorkist monarchy (see *Visual Sources,* Plate 3.3, for the crown of Edward's sister Margaret, whose marriage to the Duke of Burgundy formed an important plank of this alliance). Internecine warfare within England stood in the way of the English reclaiming their French lands.

Historians disagree about the extent to which the Wars of the Roses caused disruption, but there does seem to be a consensus that the crisis which led to them was one surrounding Henry VI's personal kingship rather than the institution of monarchy itself. Social and economic change seemed to point to a reduction in the power of the nobility vis-à-vis that of the crown over the population as a whole. Edward IV was able to reassert strong kingship and to reshape the way in which government was exercised. But weak monarchs did open the door to unrest, and there were problems deep in the structure of the English government (the constitution) that required solution before it could survive an ineffectual king. It was entirely possible for the king's council to be dominated by a few individuals. Parliament remained very weak. Other fundamental weaknesses remained: there was no machinery for legitimate, peaceable opposition, and the stability and strength of government depended entirely on the strength of the monarch. Witness what happened when Edward IV died and was succeeded by a minor.

Producers and consumers

English society was undergoing change throughout the fifteenth century. If you look back to the section on 'English society', you will see that the old hierarchy of nobility, church and commons was under considerable strain. Relations of deference were still very important but change was afoot. The Black Death relatively peacefully had loosened the ties of labour to the land and to those who owned the land. The majority of the population was still engaged in agriculture, but towns were increasingly important. In these towns (and especially in London and a few other ports) a new kind of society and government were developing in which the relationships between merchants and craftsmen, town governments and citizens were paramount. Rising lay literacy and the improved survival rates of certain types of documentation – such as family correspondence, household accounts, wills and inventories – enable historians to describe this society with some accuracy. The Vale essay showed that overseas trade was no longer dominated by France. The wool trade was in decline and the cloth trade fluctuating. The English were looking for, and finding, new markets overseas, especially in the Low Countries and the Baltic.

REFERENCES

Carpenter, C. (1992) *Locality and Polity: A Study of Warwickshire Landed Society, 1401–1499*, Cambridge, Cambridge University Press.

Carpenter, C. (1995) 'The Stonors and their circle in the fifteenth century' in Archer, R. and Walker, S. (eds) *Rulers and Ruled in Late Medieval England: Essays Presented to Gerald Harriss*, London, Hambledon Press

Carpenter, C. (ed.) (1996) *The Stonor Letters and Papers, 1290–1483*, Cambridge, Cambridge University Press, vols 1 and 2.

Carpenter, C. (1997) *The Wars of the Roses*: *Politics and the Constitution in England c.1437–1509*, Cambridge, Cambridge University Press.

Keen, M. (1973) *England in the Later Middle Ages*, London, Methuen.

Keen, M. (1990) *English Society in the Later Middle Ages, 1348–1500*, Harmondsworth, Penguin.

McFarlane, K.B. (1973) *The Nobility of Later Medieval England*, Oxford, Oxford University Press.

Rosemary O'Day

INTRODUCTION

Why have we selected beliefs and ideologies as one of the themes of this course? Historians are interested in establishing what happened in the past, in charting change, and in ascertaining cause and effect. Doing so is not simply a matter of discovering and ordering the facts, but of interpreting and explaining them as well. Why did people do what they did? Acquaintance with the mindsets or *mentalités* of people in specific contexts provides much that is of itself intriguing, but it also can provide the key to their motivation, to their acceptance of certain conditions, and to their reactions to the words or actions of others. The formal observance of religion played an enormous part in the lives of fifteenth-century men and women. It probably reflected a particular and deeply felt belief system. Its maintenance and control was seen as of crucial importance to the prosperity and survival of both secular and spiritual authorities.

The Catholic Church established and sought to maintain orthodoxy in matters of Christian doctrine (the beliefs about God and salvation that it accepted and taught), ceremonial (ritual), morals, and religious observance (worship). The late medieval churches were organised as well as ordered through the courts of their own law. (Much of what we have to say here applies in some sense to the post-Reformation Catholic and Protestant churches as well as to those of the late Middle Ages, when European churches owed allegiance to the papacy.) In Block 2 we shall emphasise the differences contingent on the early and mid-sixteenth century reformations. Here the emphasis is on late medieval Catholicism. Particular reference will be made to religion in those states that you have already studied: Burgundy, England and France. We shall be looking at this not as a mere prelude to the Reformation but as an exciting subject in its own right.

The religious beliefs of even three states form an enormously rich and complex subject. To make this study manageable, we shall concentrate on four main topics that link to the themes of the whole course – particularly the formation of the state, and beliefs and ideologies – and demonstrate the close links between the two in the fifteenth and early sixteenth centuries. The four topics are:

1   Unification by belief – to what extent were Christians unified by religious belief and worship?
2   Evidence of heresy and paganism – what evidence is there of contemporary Christian heresies and paganism?

3 Approaches to heresy and paganism – how did the church hierarchy and the secular state approach heresy and paganism? Who was sovereign within the church?

4 Control of the church – why and how did individual states fight for control over the Catholic Church in and near their territories?

A large part of the unit offers a description of mainstream religious belief and worship, on the one hand, and of heresy and paganism, on the other. We cannot go into much detail here, but we hope to give you useful and surprising insights into a worldview that was very different to our own. The written materials are provided as a backdrop for your own work of questioning original evidence (source criticism). With an eye on your workload we have restricted the number of such exercises in the text. However, if you have time, we suggest that you apply the same questioning technique to reading other anthology documents. This is a good way of ensuring that you understand the import of the various documents, which are sometimes difficult on first reading but are usually comprehensible if you persevere. Once this technique of source criticism has become second nature to you, you will employ it naturally to all your work on original evidence.

There is an emphasis in parts of the unit on the sources that historians use to enable them to describe the beliefs of fifteenth-century Europeans and to set the religious history of Burgundy, England and France in a wider context of diplomacy and state formation. We also ask you to ascertain whether the evidence is being appropriately interpreted. This emphasis relates directly to an important learning outcome of the course ('read and use appropriately a secondary source' – see the Block Introduction) While some historians engage in considerable 'source criticism' in their work, textbooks such as your set book by Wallace tend not to do so overtly. When you are reading and using a textbook, however, we want you to do so critically. Ask yourself whether the sources that the author used are likely to sustain his or her interpretation? One of the exercises below asks you to dissect a short passage from the set book by Wallace (a secondary source) from this point of view. Another asks whether we can ascertain popular religious beliefs from the kinds of evidence that survive from the fourteenth and fifteenth centuries (primary sources).

We hope that this unit will not only lead you to a greater understanding of the beliefs of fifteenth-century men and women, but also stimulate discussion of the meaning of terms such as 'belief', 'religion', 'ecclesiastical', 'church', 'heresy', 'orthodoxy' and 'state' and help you to question for yourself the terminology historians use to organise their interpretations. You will be aware by now that the study of history is a cumulative process. We hope that, as you read more, you will understand more. You have already met a definition of the 'state' in Units 1 and 2, but the work you accomplish in this unit will add a new dimension to this definition.

EXERCISE

Now read pp. 8–21 and 25–53 of the set book by Wallace. Make *brief* notes on pp. 25–53.

Spend about 1 hour on this exercise.

ORTHODOX BELIEFS

Unification by belief

To what extent were Christians unified by religious belief and worship?

The rule of the Catholic Church prevailed in all three states under consideration. There were small populations of non-Christian peoples – Jews, for example – but Islam had made little impact on these states and figures in our narrative as a perceived threat to Christendom – a threat that was met by armed crusades. The word 'catholic' means universal. Those who proclaimed it regarded the faith espoused by Catholics as universal, but in fact its organisation was restricted to parts of Europe and to European settlements and colonies overseas. (Of course, there were other branches of the Christian religion in the Middle Ages, notably the Eastern Orthodox Church.)

Liturgy (forms of public religious service)

EXERCISE

Turn to Anthology Document 1.26. Read the extracts from a recent translation of the Latin Mass that was used in the northern province of York of the church in England. Focus on the paragraph beginning 'I believe ...' and try to answer the following questions in brief note form:

1   What type of prayer is this?

2   What are the main beliefs outlined in it?

Spend about 20 minutes on this exercise.

SPECIMEN ANSWER

1   This is a declaration of beliefs known as a creed (from the Latin *credo* for 'I believe').

2   The main beliefs outlined are beliefs in: the Trinity of God the Father, God the Son and God the Holy Ghost; the virgin birth of Jesus Christ; the atoning death of Jesus on the cross; his resurrection from the dead, which saved all those who believed in him; the power of baptism to forgive sin; the idea of another life in heaven; the continuing ministry of the apostles, inspired by the Holy Spirit, and of those in the apostolic succession.

DISCUSSION

Don't worry if you have found it difficult to identify all the various points covered here, still less if you don't fully understand the concept of, for example, the Trinity.

Christians who belonged to the Catholic communion shared basic tenets of faith, as enunciated in the creed (or statement of belief). This statement (called the Nicene Creed) was said publicly in Latin on each and every Sunday of the year.

Central to this was belief in the indivisible Trinity of God the Father, God the Son and God the Holy Ghost (or Spirit). Christians believed that Christ Jesus was the son of God, who had been born of a virgin, had had a teaching ministry on earth, had suffered death on the cross to atone for the sins of the world and had been resurrected from the dead after three days to save from eternal damnation all those who believed in Him. See Figure 4.1, which shows the centrality of Christ's death (a willing sacrifice) upon the cross to the beliefs of Christians. Following his resurrection, Jesus was said to have sent the Holy Spirit to his disciples, thus commissioning the apostles (including St Paul, who never knew the living Jesus) to continue his earthly ministry. In their turn the apostles commissioned others to do this work, thus establishing what came to be known as the apostolic succession.

The pope was thought to be in the direct line of the apostolic succession through St Peter and to be the source of authority in the church, second only to the authority of Scripture and of the church fathers. Christians were taught to forsake the devil and all his works, the vanities of the wicked world, and all the so-called sinful lusts of the flesh, and to believe all the articles of the Christian faith and to keep God's holy will and commandments. During services of the church, the officiating minister (whether he be archbishop, bishop or priest) absolved (forgave) repentant sinners of their sins and administered the seven sacraments (outward and visible signs of an inward and spiritual grace) to the faithful. The seven sacraments were: Baptism, Confirmation, Marriage, Holy Orders, Penance, Communion, Holy Unction (the last rites). Christians were required to confess their sins regularly and to perform penance prior to obtaining absolution (forgiveness). See Figure 4.2, which shows Holy Week confession. During the service of the Mass it was believed that the bread and wine (or sacrament of the Eucharist or Holy Communion) blessed by the priest actually became the body and blood of Christ, the means of salvation through a process called transubstantiation. A range of other beliefs grew up surrounding those encapsulated in the creed and in the seven sacraments, but these formed the common core of western Christian faith throughout the Middle Ages and indeed extend to catholics of the present day.

Medieval accretions to the beliefs of Christians

Probably the most important of the beliefs that were added were the beliefs in purgatory, good works and associated matters. During life, active Christians could perform good works, which would act as a counterweight to their sins. Such good works included formal religious observance, attending masses, receiving the sacrament, prayer and works of charity. They also included performing pilgrimages and other works of exceptional devotion. At certain times, the popes would declare jubilee years; by making a pilgrimage to Rome in such a year a Christian would be certified to have performed a certain number of good works. Controversially, a practice arose of selling outright such indulgences, when the individual concerned was unable to perform a 'good work' (you will be looking at indulgences again in later in this unit and in Block 2). Purgatory was a place of waiting for the soul after death for those who could not be admitted immediately to heaven because they still had to discharge in some way some sins committed on earth. The accumulated merits of the saints might be invoked to assist in this discharge. It was believed that masses and prayers said by the living would act as a store of good works on which the deceased in purgatory might draw. This would speed the soul through purgatory on its way to heaven. The church was not just a building or an organisation but a communion (fellowship) of saints, both living and dead (see Figure 4.3).

Community life was based on the ecclesiastical parish and its gilds. Historians use their surviving records to reveal popular orthodox religion. Christians

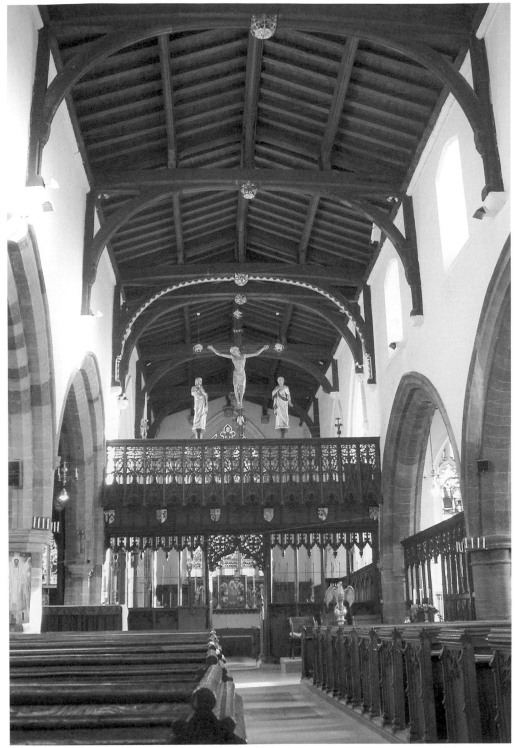

Figure 4.1   Higham Ferrers in Northamptonshire retains its rood screen and rood showing the crucifixion. This was a constant, dramatic reminder to worshippers of Christ's atoning death upon the cross, made more meaningful as they glimpsed the priest holding up the body (bread) and blood (wine) of Christ at the moment of consecration of the mass. Photo: © Mervyn Hawkins

Figure 4.2   Here we see a parish priest listening to confession during Holy Week (before Easter). Photo: Cambridge University Library

worshipped both at home and in church. Anthology Document 1.27b, records the contents of a private chapel, probably that of Thomas Stonor in 1474 (you may recall him from Unit 3). Much of what we know about household prayers and church services derives, however, from visual sources.

DVD exercise

On DVD 1, Parish Churches, we give you the opportunity to tour some surviving medieval churches and chapels that retain many of their original features. You should do this work now. You will need at least 1 hour for the activity.

DISCUSSION

Do the sources that you have studied on the DVD tell us what ordinary people of the time believed? Historians such as Eamonn Duffy, Jack Scarisbrick and Christopher Haigh think so. Have a look at the illustration of the pulpit at Strasburg in Figure 4.4 – note its instructive decorations. They also cite in support of this position evidence of the continuing popularity of parish gilds, of pilgrimages, of mystery plays and of processions.

Another view could be, however, that the church furnishings and liturgies demonstrate not so much what lay people believed as what the church wanted

Figure 4.3   All Saints' Day (1 November) was (and remains) an important feast day of the church. Here the Communion of Saints marks the opening of the text for that day in the Chevalier Hours, c. 1420. The British Library, Additional MS 16997, f. 137. Photo: The British Library

them to believe, and went to great lengths to teach them. It demonstrates what beliefs they were continually exposed to. The popularity of gilds, pilgrimages, and so on, certainly indicates a lively communal life and love of companionable travel, but does it really provide evidence of what beliefs lay people held? Anthology Document 1.30 (an extract from a churchwarden's book showing gifts made by individual parishioners to the church where they worshipped) could be used to show that these beliefs were sincerely held by lay people. However, when, in the following century, bishops tested the religious knowledge of clergy and laity, they were stunned by the general levels of ignorance of fundamentals of the faith. Whereas historians once cited the preambles of last wills and testaments to show the beliefs and allegiances of testators (See Anthology Document 2.15a–c), they now know that parishioners would more often than not use the services of their local priest or other notary or scribe to write, or help them to write, their wills. These will-writers copied forms of words from formularies. The amounts of money contributed by lay people to church furnishings and funds could have owed more to the persuasiveness of the ecclesiastical authorities, and to a desire on the part of the parishioner to conform, to memorialise a loved one or to participate in communal activities. My own view is that, while the evidence may well be indicative of popular belief, devotion and piety, it is certainly not incontrovertible.

Figure 4.4   The highly decorated late medieval pulpit at Strasburg cathedral still survives. The embellishments served a purpose of instructing and reminding Christians about the life and crucifixion of Christ, the apostles and saints. Prominent evangelical preachers such as Matthis Zell (1477–1548) preached in this pulpit asking for radical reformation. Photo: © Fondation de l'Oeuvre Notre Dame, Strasbourg

At home, the head of the household (normally the father) led family prayers attended by family members and servants. Individuals (both women and men) also were supposed to say prayers at regular intervals during the day. Books of hours were produced as sources for such prayers and meditation. (There are examples of these in the *Visual Sources* – e.g. Block 1, Plate 0.1.) Piety was often adjudged according to compliance with rules about devotion. At confession an individual would confess to the priest not only omission of good works of charity but also neglect of works of worship and ritual, and commission of sins. 'Good works' included masses sung for the dead, pilgrimages to holy places, and crusades.

The church's preoccupation with the journey to the kingdom of Heaven was made evident in the many chantry chapels. Here priests would sing masses for the souls of the departed, praying that their journey through purgatory would be shortened and made bearable. Individual Christians were encouraged on death to donate money to found such chapels and to pay for masses. (See DVD 1, The Beauchamp Chapel, Warwick.) Both crusades and pilgrimages were also regarded as good works that could help the soul on its way to salvation.

A pilgrimage was seen as a symbol of each individual's journey towards Heaven. Pilgrims from all walks of life shared a desire to visit the places associated with the lives of Christ and of his apostles, and the shrines of saints, where they would pray for favours or give thanks. The most popular pilgrimage routes were to Jerusalem in the Holy Land, to the shrine of St James at Santiago de Compostela in Spain and to Rome, but the pull of local shrines, such as those of St Thomas Becket at Canterbury and St Michael on Mont St Michel in Normandy was strong. Individual cities and churches stood to benefit enormously from the presence of pilgrims in their midst – pilgrims needed shelter, food and drink, and they were willing to pay for guide books, maps, badges and other memorabilia. (You can see one of these badges in Figure 4.5 and an illustration of early sixteenth-century pilgrims in Figure 4.6.) Rulers also took their cut. High and low subjects had to purchase licences to travel. In the 1390s, King Richard II ordered pilgrim passengers to pay him a 6d tax on their fares to Compostela, and in 1433, Henry VI levied 2d on each noble exchanged at the papal curia (the English noble was a coin worth half a mark, which in turn was worth two-thirds of a pound, or 13s 4d – around 66p). Simply going on a pilgrimage was regarded as meritorious but, increasingly, indulgences were offered, which excused pilgrims from doing penance for particular sins. This had the effect of increasing the popularity of pilgrimages. Quite often the well-to-do, who had vowed to make a pilgrimage in exchange for some favour, would perform proxy pilgrimages – paying substitutes to go on the pilgrimage for them, willing an obligation to pilgrimage to a descendant or paying a fine instead. Master Thomas Polton, Bishop of Worcester, who had spent much of his career as Henry V's representative at the papal curia (or court) left money in his will of 1433 to pay for a chaplain to live in Rome for two years, visiting all the shrines and holy places and saying masses for the donor's soul (Labarge, 2005, pp. 81–113).

Figure 4.5   Leaden pilgrim badges in the form of the head of Thomas Becket, from the shrine at Canterbury. Pilgrims bore resemblances to modern tourists but badges also provided evidence that an individual had performed 'good work'. Photo: © Museum of Canterbury

EXERCISE

One of the best-documented noble pilgrimages of the fifteenth century was that undertaken by the earl of Warwick (remember him from Unit 3), who was commemorated by the Beauchamp Chapel (see DVD 1) and illustrated in a series of 53 line drawings in the *Pageant of the Birth, Life and Death of Richard de Beauchamp, Earl of Warwick* (British Library Cotton Julius E.iv). Examine the line drawings that are supplied electronically on the course website and Plates 3.4 and 3.5 in the *Visual Sources*. What can you see in these drawings? What part did pilgrimage play in Beauchamp's life? How can we generalise from his experience to that of the fifteenth-century nobility? Answer briefly.

Spend about 25 minutes on this exercise.

Figure 4.6   Pilgrims leaving Canterbury (*c.*1525), an addition by a Flemish artist (*c* 1525) to an unfinished copy of John Lydgate's poems, *c* 1465. The British Library, Royal MS 18 D ii, f. 148. Photo: The British Library

SPECIMEN ANSWER

Here, an English nobleman, Richard de Beauchamp, earl of Warwick, is shown making a pilgrimage through France, Italy and the Holy Land in the early fifteenth century. This helps us to understand how such pilgrimages were conducted. Beauchamp, for example, visited the French court and he also participated in secular activities, such as a joust, on his way to Venice. It also indicates that commitment to pilgrimage existed among the nobility. It is interesting that Beauchamp was recording his performance of the pilgrimage by having his coat of arms displayed near the shrine of the Holy Sepulchre. It was a 'good work' which counted towards the earl's salvation.

DISCUSSION

This series of drawings, probably made in the 1480s or 1490s, shows Richard setting off for France in his pilgrim's gown and cap in 1408, meeting his French cousin, the duke of Bar, and travelling with him to the French court to be entertained. He was then provided with a herald, who saw him safely across France to Italy. In Italy he participated in a joust at Verona, visited the inn of St George at Venice and obtained a galley to make the journey to Jaffa and back again. Once in Jerusalem, he was entertained by the Christian patriarch before making his pilgrimage to the Holy Sepulchre. Interestingly, his coat of arms was hung on the north side of the shrine as evidence of his visit. The late date of this pageant book should be noted – although there is no reason to suppose that it is inaccurate, it was produced some 70–80 years after the events it described, probably commissioned by Beauchamp's daughter Anne (Beauchamp) Neville or his grand-daughter Anne Neville to demonstrate her pedigree.

When the pilgrimage was over, the earl went on to Prussia to engage in a crusade. Crusades were less important in the fourteenth and fifteenth centuries than in the thirteenth. The fourteenth century saw the crusading movement shift from Palestine to Prussia and Lithuania, where the Order of Teutonic Knights accepted the assistance of young knights from England, France and elsewhere in Europe to enforce Christianity. While the kings of France and England could not countenance supporting crusades in the Holy Land, which would draw their armies away from their secular struggles during the Hundred Years War, the crusade to Prussia served a valuable purpose during periods of truce of keeping young and restless knights occupied. Richard de Beauchamp's crusading venture in 1408–9 can be seen as part of this trend. The late fourteenth and early fifteenth centuries saw another change in focus – crusades were to be launched against the Turks. The dukes of Burgundy were undoubtedly enthusiastic about the prospect and knights still made crusading vows but, apart from a few skirmishes, the crusades came to little.

In church, a priest led worship on Sundays and Holy Days. Figure 4.7 shows the priest in his mass vestments with his back to the people. Plates 7.8 and 7.9 in the *Visual Sources* show him lavishly dressed for high mass. A Latin liturgy provided by the Catholic Church was used. Latin was the language of the literate throughout Europe, although by the later Middle Ages it was rivalled by the vernacular. The main services of the church were matins (morning) and vespers (evening) and the Mass. The uneducated relied on popular vernacular preaching, on visual aids (such as stained glass windows, rood screens, altar pieces and wall paintings), and on drama and processions (such as mystery plays and tableaux) to explain and reinforce the Christian message. Plate 4.7 shows the emergence in the later part of the period of vernacular religious texts, indicating a growing demand by a literate laity for books of religious instruction. Take a look now at Figures 4.4, 4.8–4.10, which show some of these visual and dramatic aids. Figure 4.7 shows the emergence in the later part of the period of vernacular religious texts, indicating a growing demand by a literate laity for books of religious instruction. See also *Visual Sources*, Plates 4.1 and 4.2.

While the Latin liturgy served to unify Christians in worship, there were many locally distinctive features and fashions in popular religious culture. For example, in England, devotion to the Virgin Mary was especially popular in the fourteenth century, but in the fifteenth century was overtaken by devotion to the name of Jesus; this devotion found its chief expression in the establishment of parish gilds in his name. In Strasburg, cults of the Virgin Mary were dominant in the fifteenth century.

Figure 4.7   This Flemish book of hours, dated *c.*1492, shows the priest celebrating mass, with his back to the congregation. Note that all clergy, whether seculars (priests and deacons) or regulars (monks and friars), were differentiated from laity by both ceremonial and daily dress and by the tonsure (shaved patch) on the crown of the head. In church the clergy were physically set apart from the laity. British Library, Additional MS 25698, f. 2. Photo: The British Library

Figure 4.8 An Easter sepulchre at Heckingham, Lincolnshire, commemorating the resurrection of Christ. It would have reinforced dramatically the central Easter story. National Monuments Record, BB62/785. Photo: © English Heritage

Figure 4.9   The font (placed at the normal entrance to the church) symbolised the initiation of the Christian through the first sacrament of baptism. This one at Little Walsingham, Norfolk, illustrated all seven sacraments (see also Plate 4.1). National Monuments Record, A42/7192. Photo: © English Heritage

Figure 4.10   Even the wooden seats in churches were used to remind congregations of the seven deadly sins. This one at Blythburgh, Suffolk, shows hypocrisy or pride. National Monuments Record, A48/7059. Photo: © English Heritage

Summary

So far we have seen that western Christendom was unified by a belief system based in part on Scripture and the Nicene Creed and in part on ideas about salvation that had been added during the Middle Ages. Some, but not all, of these beliefs had papal approval.

HERESIES AND PAGANISM

Evidence of heresy and paganism

In present-day Britain, most people are not interested in, or are opposed to, organised religion and imposed belief (there are, of course, exceptions). Moreover, although there is an official state church, the state tolerates other belief systems and it is accepted that people have the right to determine what they believe and to practise their religion, as long as they do not break the law of the land or incite others to do so. In the fifteenth century, however, it was considered unthinkable by both secular and spiritual authorities that people should be allowed to reject Christianity or to modify its creed. In fact, it has been described as essentially an age of orthodoxy and of devotion that somewhat strangely produced the reformations of the sixteenth century. It is important for us to think ourselves into the mindset that prevailed – a mindset that gripped the part of northern Europe with which we are here concerned until well into the eighteenth century. Inevitably we shall focus on the few heresies that were uncovered by the 'thought police' of the time and did have some impact on contemporary belief, but we should not exaggerate the importance of the Waldensian, Hussite and Lollard movements themselves. However, these 'heresies' do demonstrate how easy it was for ordinary men and women to modify the official creed of the church. We should remember also that, while the Catholic authorities, both secular and spiritual, did define and occasionally confront heresy, they also effected a compromise with surviving elements of paganism that permitted people to embrace Christianity even though they clung to aspects of the old religion.

In the fifteenth century, the possibility of unbelief was not countenanced by either the church or the secular authorities. Orthodoxy was laid down and those who strayed from it were often persecuted as heretics. The period 1400–1500 was not the age of heretics. By 1400, the most formidable opponents of orthodoxy – the Cathars (or Albigensians) of the south – had been extirpated. The Catharist heresy held a belief in the existence of two opposing principles, if not two deities, of good and evil – God and Satan. This dualism opposed a pure spiritual world with a carnal, physical, corrupt, terrestrial world. Believers were divided between the elite *parfait* (who, once initiated, had to remain pure and abstain from both sex and meat) and the *credentes*, or simple believers. It was easy for such beliefs to take hold because they were an exaggeration and misunderstanding of orthodox Christian beliefs in both God and the Devil. By about 1200, Catharism had reached large parts of Languedoc and a crusade was organised by the northern French barons against the heresy. In 1244, the last heretic fortress was taken but Catharism continued in the mountainous regions of southern France. There was even a revival in the early fourteenth century that centred on the village of Montaillou in upper Ariège. This last pocket of heresy was flushed out by an inquisition staged by Jacques Fournier, bishop of Pamiers, between 1318 and 1325. Fournier later became Pope Benedict XII.

Although all this happened well before our period, it is worth noting for several reasons. First, the dualistic beliefs of the Cathars did have parallels in our period and in the views of some sixteenth-century religious radicals. Second, although in the popular mind the term 'inquisition' conjures up the sixteenth-century Spanish Inquisition, in fact the inquisition was part of the normal but relatively rarely used disciplinary apparatus of the medieval Catholic Church. In this case, Fournier set up his own inquisitorial tribunal to reveal the existence of heresy by means of detailed and skilful questioning. He dealt with heretics by various means – sometimes including burning at the stake. When Joan of Arc was handed over to the ecclesiastical authorities, much the same procedure was used to uncover her beliefs and determine their orthodoxy.

The Waldensian heresy of the Middle Ages was less spectacular but much more resilient than the Catharist. Its founder was supposedly a Lyons merchant called Waldo or Valdes who, consumed with anxiety for the state of his soul, sold all his goods, distributed the proceeds to the poor, and gathered about him a movement of pious, ascetic lay people. The Waldenses taught using the partial vernacular translations of the Scriptures, regarded the visible church as corrupt and preached a puritanical and pacific gospel. They were typical of groups who pressed for a return to the primitive simplicity of the early church – groups such as the followers of John Wycliffe (Lollards or Wycliffites) in England and the followers of John Hus (Hussites) in Bohemia (what was later to become Czechoslovakia). In 1369, the persecution of the Waldensians in the Alps began with the creation of an inquisition and subsequent crusades during the later fourteenth century. In the 1480s, the ferocity of the persecution intensified after a period of relative calm. Archbishop Jehan Baile took up the cudgel in earnest once more in Vallouise and Fressinières, using inquisition, mass excommunication and armed crusade. Two major assaults – one Catholic and one Protestant – were made on the integrity of the Waldenses in the period 1480–1580: an armed crusade in winter 1487 that ravaged several villages; and later ideological assault by the Swiss Protestants to convert the Waldenses to their discipline. These were interspersed with intermittent persecution.

The motivation behind such persecution was not always clear. Local clergy seem to have been genuinely anxious to discover the reason for the heretic's error and to persuade him or her to embrace orthodoxy. Inquisitorial 'visitors' from outside the areas involved seemed more concerned to achieve rapid results and to find the excuse for a crusade. After a crusade, visitors commuted penances for money, levied fines and ransoms, and sold confiscated lands. A crusade was often a profitable proposition for the authorities.

Lollards and Lollardy

EXERCISE

Read Anthology Document 1.28 about Lollards in the diocese of Coventry.

What beliefs and practices are revealed in these depositions? What types of people are involved? Answer in note form.

Spend about 40 minutes on this exercise.

SPECIMEN ANSWER

- Objections to the sacrament of the altar (now known as the Mass, Eucharist or Holy Communion, or the Lord's Supper). These either imply or state outright a belief that the Lord's Supper was a matter of remembrance only and not of the real presence of Christ in the bread and wine. (See Deposition of Thomas Bowne of Coventry and of Joan Smyth of Coventry.)

- Objections to pilgrimages.

- Objections to the veneration of saints and to making offerings to saints.

- Reading (or listening to readings from) the vernacular Scriptures.

- Consorting with other heretics (see Deposition of John Atkinson). Allegations are made that the women actively recruit to their beliefs. (See examination of Thomas Browne.)

- The people involved inhabit Coventry or its surrounding parishes but refer to a wider group – in Leicester, for instance. They include men and women largely drawn from the artisan and merchant community and falling in the age group 40–60. Some people who could be clergy or gentry are also implicated by Robert Hachet.

DISCUSSION

The English Lollards (or Wycliffites) followed the teachings of a fourteenth-century Oxford academic, John Wycliffe (d.1384). The teachings emphasised access to the Word of God through the vernacular Scriptures and contested some fundamental Catholic teachings and practices, especially the efficacy of the sacrament of the Eucharist or Lord's Supper (celebrated at the Mass) and of the mediation of saints. Take a look at Figure 4.11, which shows the veneration of the Virgin Mary, a practice that Lollards abhorred. For adoration of the Virgin, see also *Visual Sources*, Plate 4.3. (This was in fact balanced by an emphasis on the suffering Christ. See Plate 4.4.)

Until the second decade of the fifteenth century, this was a largely academic movement. In that decade, however, Oxford was purged of the heretics and Sir John Oldcastle, a Lollard knight, led an unsuccessful (and brutally suppressed) revolt against the crown. Lollardy then went underground and became primarily a lay movement that seems to have appealed to working people in most counties of southern England. Books and reading were an important part of their communal life. It was very much a minority movement, but in a few towns and villages this minority was both large and influential. The thriving city of Coventry was one of these places. Bishop John Hales of Coventry and Lichfield brought heresy prosecutions against a group of Coventry Lollards in 1486. Lollardy continued to thrive there, however, and in 1511, after occasional attempts to clamp down on the movement, Bishop Geoffrey Blyth of the same diocese made a more determined effort to destroy the Coventry Lollards (McSheffrey and Tanner, 2003, pp. 1–55). The accused were imprisoned at the Augustinian priory at Maxstoke, Warwickshire, and the trials, which took several months, were held by the bishop in person until 25 January 1512, accompanied by eight or nine senior clergy – a mark of the

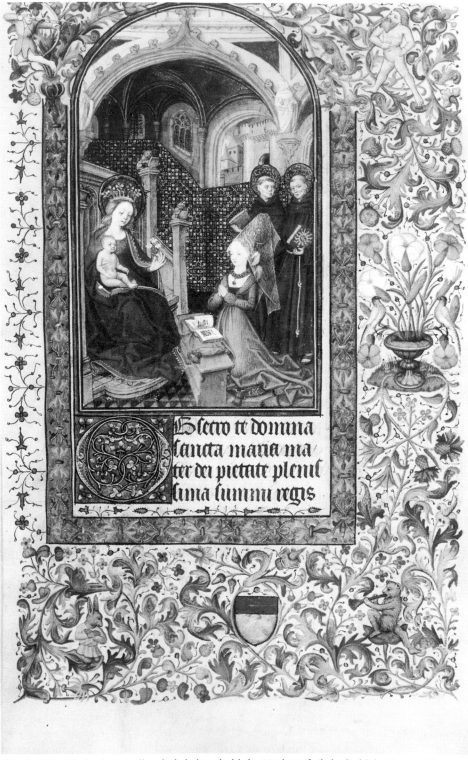

Figure 4.11 Orthodox medieval Christians held the Mother of Christ in high esteem. The owner of this book of hours for private prayer had herself portrayed kneeling at her feet. British Library, Additional MS 27697, f. 19. Photo: The British Library

seriousness with which this alleged heresy was regarded. The final trials, however, took place before a specially appointed commission. The Lollards were forced to abjure their heresy and to do public penance, wearing only undergarments and carrying heavy faggots of wood; one of them, Joan Warde alias Wasshingburn, was burned to death. Yet there is evidence that the Coventry group still persisted. For example, John Foxe, a martyrologist in Elizabeth I's reign, reported that seven of the group were re-arrested in 1520. As relapsed heretics they were burned to death in April 1520. (Please note further reading in secondary sources for this unit.)

How many people in England shared Lollard beliefs? It is impossible to give an accurate estimate of the number of Lollards. We know that it was more popular in some areas than in others, that it survived in Yorkshire and the Chilterns, for example, until the sixteenth century, and that it appealed especially to artisans. Its importance as indicative of widespread popular beliefs in England in the fifteenth century has probably been overstated because, retrospectively, it seemed to historians that Lollardy presaged early Protestant beliefs so that it seemed like 'the morning star of the reformation'. Inclusion of cases brought against Lollards in the 1563 edition of John Foxe's *Acts and Monuments* indicates the way in which Protestants laid claim to the Lollards and their beliefs. (See Anthology Document 1.29.)

Summary

Not all men and women who said they were Christians adhered to the orthodox belief system. Heresy was probably not *statistically* very important in the fifteenth century, but its links with reforming movements of the late fifteenth and sixteenth centuries give it a different kind of importance.

Approaches to heresy and paganism

In this section we shall consider how the church hierarchy and the secular state approached heresy and paganism, and who was sovereign within the church.

Orthodoxy – what is it?

How did the church decide what was a heresy?

> Heresy is defined by reference to orthodoxy. It does not exist alone. A doctrine [teaching] or a sect becomes heretical when condemned as such by the Church. For this there has to be a body of accepted beliefs to violate and a recognised authority to enforce it.
>
> (Leff, 1967, vol. 1, p. 1)

The people and institutions responsible for defining orthodoxy and, therefore, heresy were popes, cardinals, archbishops and bishops, general councils, universities and inquisitorial offices.

Orthodoxy was further defined as and when these arbiters of belief intervened to uncover, condemn and suppress particular heretical beliefs (e.g. in 1383, the archbishop of Canterbury condemned Wycliffite ideas in England; in 1418,

Pope Martin V condemned the views of both Wycliffe and Hus). There is a negative flavour to the definition of belief – the emphasis was on which views should not be held, as well as on which should prevail. The bodies concerned proceeded to restate official belief.

The Conciliar Movement

General councils of the church, such as those at Pisa (1409), Constance (1414–18) and Basel (1431/2), backed by universities, and that of Paris, in particular, originated solemn definitions of heretical belief and orthodoxy. Their power and authority as representatives of the voice of the universal church had been mooted during the Great Schism (when, for forty years between 1378 and 1417, there were two popes – one at Avignon in France and one at Rome). The Conciliar Movement was an oligarchic revolution occasioned by the schism. The cardinals called a council at Pisa in 1409, independently of both popes. In 1414–18, the council of Constance assembled and asserted both the supremacy of ecumenical synods such as theirs and the theory that such synods should be summoned regularly and frequently. Conciliar theory proved a direct threat to papal ascendancy. The council of Constance not only deposed the (by then) three existing popes and installed a new one, it also declared that the pope was obliged to obey a general council in matters of faith, the extinction of the schism and the reform of the church in its head and members. The council of Basel aired opinions even more radical, electing its own anti-pope. Ironically, after the reunification of the papacy with the election of Pope Martin V as pope in 1417, councils lost their ascendancy but continued to be called (Pavia, 1423; Basel, 1432; Florence, 1439). By the end of the fifteenth century, the Conciliar Movement was defeated and the papacy had regained the upper hand. The close association of the theology faculties of the universities with conciliarism meant that, during the later fifteenth and sixteenth centuries, they were ignored by the papacy or seen as a threat to the universal church. The papacy recovered some of its prestige from negotiations at Ferrara and Florence (1438–9) with the Greek Orthodox Church, which achieved short-lived unity in Christendom. In 1460, Pope Pius II, a former liberal humanist and enthusiast for conciliarism named Aeneas Piccolomini, felt able to declare heretical any and every appeal to a general council. Despite this, popes throughout the remainder of the fifteenth century and the entire sixteenth century remained highly sensitive to any suggestion of the revival of conciliarism.

The most ardent advocates of the authority of councils were anxious to demonstrate that this did not lessen their concern for the faith and the preservation of orthodoxy. John Hus was brought to Constance in 1414, tried in 1415 by the council, and condemned as a heretic when he refused to recant all his beliefs. Instead, Hus urged that he should be shown the falsity of his beliefs by reference to the Scriptures. He was handed over to the secular authorities in 1415 and executed. The same commission also inquired into Wycliffite beliefs.

The Conciliar Movement was keen to assert its own authority within the church vis-à-vis the papacy. By refusing to recant his opinions when the council condemned them, Hus was assuming for himself the right to be his own judge on matters of belief, subject to a scriptural test, and denying the council's right and authority to dictate to the faithful what they should believe.

Many of the debates of the period can be reduced to debates about the location of authority in matters of belief.

EXERCISE

Read pp. 54–63 of the set book by Wallace and make brief notes. Think about what you have read so far in this unit and try to answer the question: Where did the following believe that authority lay?

1   Lollards, Hussites and Waldensians.

2   General councils.

3   Popes.

4   Secular rulers.

Spend about 1 hour on this exercise.

SPECIMEN ANSWER

1   Ultimate authority lies in the Scriptures as the Word of God. The authority of popes, councils and the church on earth is acknowledged only when it is demonstrably consistent with the Word of God.

2   General councils saw themselves as having the ultimate authority.

3   Popes saw things differently – they possessed ultimate authority. If there were general councils, then the popes called these and their authority was delegated by him.

4   Secular rulers had a degree of ambivalence in their attitude to the authority of the papacy as played out in the territorial churches. During the Great Schism it was advantageous for the French king to have a pope in Avignon. Mostly secular rulers were concerned to control patronage to ecclesiastical appointments in their lands and to benefit from ecclesiastical taxation.

DISCUSSION

For Lollards, Hussites and Waldensians, the individual interprets the Scriptures and obeys the dictates of the church only in so far as they are consistent with Scripture.

General councils did see themselves as the ultimate authority, although they acknowledged the authority of the popes as leaders and representatives of the church on earth; of the early church fathers and of tradition; as well as of Scripture, interpreted by the clergy.

The popes revered the traditions of the church, as embodied in the works of the early church fathers, and the Word of God, as embodied in the Holy Bible, but they saw themselves as imbued with authority through the apostolic succession and as the final arbiters of belief.

While secular rulers avowed their orthodoxy, they nonetheless did not hesitate to challenge the papal right to intervene in the internal affairs of their states in the interests of preserving Catholic orthodoxy of faith and practice. Take a look at Figure 4.12, which shows Christians bringing first fruits into church. When the papacy pressed its claims to authority too far, and in a way that seemed to impinge on the sovereign's power and authority in both secular and spiritual affairs, a prince might

Figure 4.12   Peasants bring offerings to the parson. Bishops paid their first fruits to the pope. In England under Henry VIII, this became contentious. British Library, Additional MS 20787, f. 104 v. Photo: The British Library

be forced to break relations with the papacy. (This was to be seen in its most familiar and starkest form in the case of King Henry VIII of England's divorce from Queen Catharine of Aragon, to which we shall return in the next block.)

Summary

To sum up, the question of who defined orthodoxy (and who was sovereign) within the Catholic Church led to a struggle between popes, councils and, to some extent, local rulers. In some situations this could lead to a showdown about the location of sovereignty in secular (temporal) states.

CONTROL OF THE CHURCH: SECULAR VS SPIRITUAL AUTHORITIES

Why and how did individual states fight for control over the Catholic Church in and near their territories? One of the main themes of this unit is the formation of the state, and the ways in which religion and ecclesiastical affairs impinged on it. You should note that this was not simply a matter of defining the geographical boundaries of the state. Equally important was the question of where sovereignty lay within it. In Unit 3 we noted that, within England, the institution of kingship was strong and other institutions – such as parliament – weak. It is not possible to conclude, however, that the king of England was sovereign in the English state, because in many ways the loyalties of his subjects were divided. English monarchs were aware of this. What was true of England was true elsewhere in this respect.

What was a state in the fifteenth century? We should be careful not to confuse the territorial possessions of medieval monarchs with what are today known as nation states. For good reasons the territories that belonged to a specific sovereign were known as kingdoms, duchies and principalities. While some territories had long traditions of allegiance or 'belonging' to a given monarch (for example, England to the king of England after 1066) others shifted allegiance, whether voluntarily or forcibly, with some frequency. Border lands often had uncertain loyalties: this was apparent in quite modern times in Nice (Italy/France) and Alsace (Germany/France). Locality meant more to the inhabitants of some areas than did the rule of a distant sovereign; this was a situation that pertained, for example, in some parts of France where French was not widely spoken, well into the nineteenth century.

We need also to ponder the attitude that kings, dukes and other rulers had to their states. While it is true that sovereigns sought to expand and consolidate their lands and to exercise rule over them, this was not in general from any feeling of obligation to the people of these lands or any sense that they 'belonged to one another'. Sovereigns sought power, influence and wealth, and land represented all three. Sovereigns needed wealth to support their families, households and burgeoning bureaucracies. (Remember what Fortescue had to say about the complexity of the English king's household and the demands it made on him – Anthology Document 1.22.) Losing lands that had long been ruled by a dynasty robbed that dynasty of the wherewithal to maintain itself and its place in the polity of Europe. Patriotic feeling played little or no part in their thinking.

Today we write of the executive servants of the state as the government and of its administrative arm as the civil service, but in medieval times these servants were not the state's but the king's. When Philip the Good or Charles the Bold of Burgundy (see Unit 2) sought ecclesiastical positions for their kin and servants, they were not so much seeking to extend their 'state' as to support these dependants at little or no cost to themselves, to protect their lands and revenues, and to extend their own influence on the European stage.

The relationships between territorial and ecclesiastical rulers were symbiotic. The obvious motivations were frequently not the only ones. The principality and city of Liège were strategically important because of its position on the river Meuse, one of the arteries of Burgundian trade, and its common interests with other powerful Burgundian cities, such as Ghent. As well as being a churchman, the bishop of Liège was the ruler of a principality. He was involved in disputes with the major city of his diocese, Liège. The dukes of Burgundy were tempted to intervene.

In 1456, with papal consent, Philip secured the appointment of his 18-year-old nephew Louis de Bourbon as bishop. But Louis's subjects rebelled and the young bishop fled to exile in Maastricht in the same year. Louis appealed to Philip for help and his subjects appealed to the king of France. Between 1461 and 1463, both tried to act as intermediaries. From 1461 to 1468, the city government was fought over by groups who sought an accommodation with the bishop and the dukes of Burgundy and those who opposed them. The dukes of Burgundy launched four campaigns. That of August 1466 ended with the Treaty of Oleye, by which the Liègeois had to accept Philip the Good as hereditary guardian. That of 1467 ended with the abolition of the law courts and imposition of written laws. The Liègeois revolted in 1468 and Duke Charles the Bold's response was a devastating sack of the city. In asserting control over Liège, the dukes of Burgundy showed themselves as powerful secular rulers and as protectors of the church.

| EXERCISE |

Turn to *Visual Sources*, Plate 4.5.

Take a few minutes to observe and note down the principal elements of the votive statue (or *ex voto*). Note the materials and the date. Why do you think it is interesting in the context of the above discussion?

Spend about 10 minutes on this exercise.

| SPECIMEN ANSWER |

This votive statue was made of gold. There are three elements: the kneeling figure of Charles, the figure of St George and a reliquary (container for a holy relic) held by Duke Charles. This statue was commissioned in 1467 but was not presented to the cathedral of Liège until 1471. The production of the statue appears to be linked with the events in Liège, especially the Burgundian campaigns of 1467 and 1468.

| DISCUSSION |

This statue was made by the ducal goldsmith and valet, Gerard Loyet. A scholar named Hugo van der Velden studied the *ex voto*. He suggested that Duke Charles first contemplated commissioning a simple statue of himself after his entry into Liège in November 1467 when he made an offering to St Lambert, the patron saint of the city and cathedral. It was quite common for rulers to offer votive statues at shrines, although this one was unusual in its cost and elaborateness. Van der Velden argued that Charles decided on a more elaborate statue after the revolt of Liège in 1468. At this point he probably decided to include St George (rather than, as one might expect, St Lambert) as a sign of Charles's lifelong devotion to St George and possibly in fulfilment of a vow that he had made to present a statue of St George if granted victory over the Liègeois. Did you make a link between the production of the statue and the events in Liège? If so, well done. Artefacts can add a further dimension to our understanding of the links between religion and the power and authority of princes.

The reliquary perhaps originally held a relic of St Adrian. During the 1468 campaign, churches had been sacked and relics of saints, including St Adrian, seized. The statue would probably have been placed near the altar and acted as a permanent reminder of the duke's role as protector of the church. Charles was eager to enforce a papal edict ordering the restitution (return) of ecclesiastical goods. Van der Velden, however, thinks that this is an image of Duke Charles's power and authority as well as of his piety and religious role. The duke was regent of the city and the precious metal used to make the statue demonstrated his power and wealth. It was also a symbol of his role as protector of the church, and of the bishop and bishopric of Liège, and the implied approval of the cathedral's patron, St Lambert. It 'bore witness to Charles's firm conviction of the legitimacy and righteousness of his actions' (van der Velden, 2000, pp. 152–3).

The Great Schism

In 1303, at a time when the papacy seemed all-powerful in western Christendom, King Philip IV of France, whom Pope Boniface VIII had been about to excommunicate, stormed the papal palace at Anagni, Italy, and took Pope Boniface VIII captive. Between 1303 and 1378, there was a pope in Avignon, France (Clement V, John XXII, Clement VI, Urban V and Gregory XI) who was, in effect, a puppet of the French king. Then, after the election of Urban VI as pope in Rome and the election of Pope Clement VII as pope in Avignon, Catholic Christendom was split into two until 1417, in what came to be called The Great Schism.

What does this have to do with our main themes? Well, the capture of the papacy by France was the result of a long struggle for French control over the territorial church in France, which was echoed by similar (if rather less obviously confrontational) struggles in England and other states. Monarchs claimed the right to make senior ecclesiastical appointments and to tax the clergy regularly. In 1302, Pope Boniface VIII had issued his bull *Unam Sanctam*, which laid out the whole theory of papal theocracy (government by God). Throughout the fourteenth and fifteenth centuries this concept was contested. Christendom was clearly not unified. General councils of the church (in what is called by historians the Conciliar Movement) brought the schism to an end and, at the council of Constance, brought about partial reform of papal abuses and took action against heresy, notably that of John Hus in Bohemia. The popes at Rome initially stood by a promise to rule with councils, but the council at Basel in 1431/2 was the last to meet outside Italy. Pope Pius II reclaimed sovereignty over the whole church (including councils) with his bull *Execrabilis* in 1460. The papacy rapidly became once more an Italian institution. This fed into a continuing struggle for territorial control of local churches.

Popes and rulers

The Italian medieval and Renaissance popes were forced to play a diplomatic game during the fifteenth century and early sixteenth century in which they did not necessarily have the upper hand. As a result they were frequently willing to accommodate the local ambitions of Christian kings. For instance, in the English concordat of 1418, Pope Martin V rewarded Henry V for his support during the council of Constance and for the promise of his future support against conciliarist claims by officially recognising the effective control that the English monarch exercised over the English church. In the 1420s, Martin tried to win back control over English ecclesiastical appointments but, during Henry VI's reign, the papacy eventually conceded defeat. When Henry VII established himself on the throne, the papacy was willing once again to reach an accommodation in the interests of international political support, which allowed Henry VII control over senior appointments and church income.

In attending to the theme of the formation of the state, we need to consider the location of sovereignty (shorthand for ultimate authority and power) within the state and how this was established. As Figure 4.13 indicates, the church was thought to legitimate and sanctify royal authority, but relations between church and state were more complicated than that. See also Plates 3.2 and 4.6, which show the piety and the legitimised authority of English royalty. As suggested above, popes and monarchs were involved in what amounted to an elaborate game of chess in this regard – this sometimes involved outright confrontation but, more often, it was a process of negotiation. To the historian, this presents a challenge of its own because the players rarely stated their ultimate goal or their game plan. I have selected one extended example – that of Burgundy – to show how *involved* the relationship between the temporal and spiritual authorities in a state could be. (You don't need to remember the detail.)

Philip the Good's relations with the papacy

Philip the Good of Burgundy achieved similar benefits to those won by Henry V of England when he lent his support to the papacy. The episode of the conflict between Pope Eugenius IV and the council of Basel is worthy of our attention. Under Eugenius's predecessor, Martin V, Burgundy had already supported the papal claims to ultimate authority. When Eugenius summoned the council of the church at Basel, the Burgundian prelate was the first of the very few to arrive in 1431. Eugenius speedily began to cement the Burgundian alliance by recognising Philip as ruler of his territories and by promising to help him in the struggle with the Emperor Sigismund over lands in the Low Countries. At first Philip pursued a cautious line of neutrality and conciliation, although the Burgundian insistence on precedence in the seating arrangements at Basel certainly had the effect of delaying proceedings. The conflict between the pope and the church fathers escalated in the years 1431–3. In 1431, the pope officially dissolved the council, but the council announced that it could not be summarily dismissed in this way. Philip the Good did what he could to use diplomacy to bring the two sides together, while maintaining a very

Figure 4.13   The blessing of the French royal banners at Charles V of France's coronation in 1365 symbolised the church's legitimisation of royal authority, from the coronation book of Charles V of France, 1365. British Library, Cotton MS Tiberius viii, f. 73. Photo: The British Library

cautious line. 'He had been just as ready to request or accept favours from Basel, as from the pope' (Vaughan, 2002, p. 215): in September 1433 he sent a larger embassy to the council which promised Burgundian support for the council's programme of reform but, fearing a further schism in the church, urged the council to withdraw its decree against the papacy for a period of three months, during which they should seek reconciliation or Philip would withdraw his support. Eugenius IV responded by promoting several of Philip's servants to prominent ecclesiastical places – the sees of Chalon and Tournai and benefices in Utrecht and Chartres. He also sent a 'host' (a piece of communion bread or wafer) to Philip at Dijon; this particular 'host' was reputed to be a piece of the actual body of Christ that had been pierced by a Jew and hence was miraculously blood-stained. This drew pilgrims from throughout his dukedom and became a valuable source of revenue. When the council directly opposed the preferment of Burgundian candidates to the sees of Trier, Utrecht and Tournai, the alliance between pope and duke was further strengthened. The council lost influence as secular rulers feared the onset of another schism and removed their representatives. The pope called a council at Ferrara. Philip the Good forbade the sale of indulgences granted by the council of Basel in his lands, thus striking at its financial infrastructure. He assembled his clergy at Arras in January 1438 to discuss the conflict between council and pope. Then he sent an embassy comprising Jehan Germain and others who had formerly represented him at Basel to the pope's council in Ferrara. This strengthened Eugenius's claim that he had transferred the council from Basel to Ferrara and that the rump remaining in Basel had no legitimacy. In 1439, the council of Ferrara was transferred to Florence to avoid the plague. In November 1439, the emasculated council at Basel took the dramatic step of electing a new pope – the former duke of Savoy, Amadeus VIII, who was in fact Philip the Good's uncle. Philip, however, did not swerve from his loyalty to Eugenius. He prevented the circulation of indulgences, pardons and other documents emanating from Basel. He even created a Burgundian fleet to assist in Eugenius's planned crusade to the Holy Land. Eugenius again rewarded him: the pope issued a dispensation to allow Philip's illegitimate student brother Jehan de Bourgogne to become bishop of Cambrai; he gave the Duchess Isabel the right to appoint to twelve church benefices; he allowed a licence for the marriage of Charles of Orleans to Mary of Cleves. Then he signed two concordats with Philip (6 November 1441 and 23 April 1442) that restricted papal powers to make ecclesiastical appointments within those of Philip's territories that lay outside France and limited appeals from these lands to Rome. These provisions were similar to those agreed in the Pragmatic Sanction of Bourges in 1439 with respect to French territories. In 1441, Eugenius accorded Philip the right to levy a tax of one-tenth on all the clerical lands in his territories.

| EXERCISE |

The extract below is taken from *Chronique, 1440–1449* by Jehan de Stavelot, a monk of Liège, which is a contemporary chronicle that interprets the motivations behind a papal grant. Read the extract and make brief notes on the benefits that Philip the Good and Pope Eugenius IV extracted from their alliance, and on the motivations attributed by the contemporary observer to the pope in granting Philip the right to levy tenths.

> You should understand the reason why our holy father the pope granted this favour to the duke of Burgundy. The forgoing bull states that it was because he made peace in France and had helped to win over the Greeks ... But the main reason, which is not mentioned in the bull, was to encourage him to help and support Pope Eugenius against the Council of Basel and its partisans. For the same reason Pope Eugenius permitted the Duke, during his lifetime, to collate to all benefices throughout his lands. The pope was much criticised for gifts of this kind.
>
> (de Stavelot, 1861)

Spend about 10 minutes on this exercise.

- The pope claimed that he was granting this favour because of Philip's help in securing peace in France and winning Greek support for himself.

- Jehan pinpoints a deeper motivation: securing Philip's support against the Basel council and its supporters.

- In return, Philip was given the right to collate (appoint) to ecclesiastical benefices and to tax the clergy.

Contemporary chroniclers such as Jehan de Stavelot provide historians with additional material regarding the symbiotic relationships between secular rulers and the papacy. The chronicler copied out the terms of the papal grant of taxation to Philip. He also added his own commentary on the pope's motivation and other grants he made to Philip.

Eugenius's actions in 1446 represented the apogee of his generosity to Philip. He deposed Philip's opponents from the archbishoprics of Cologne and Trier and replaced them with Philip's relatives: his nephew Adolf of Cleves to Cologne and his bastard brother Jehan de Bourgogne to Trier. The uproar that this caused with the electors and with the Holy Roman Emperor Frederick III caused Eugenius to reverse his decision and reinstate the original archbishops. Philip was content to accept this situation because he had no wish to be embroiled in war.

It must not be supposed that the pope could always easily reward his supporters. The struggle between Burgundy and France for the strategically important see of Tournai was a case in point. The city of Tournai on the river Schelde formed a French enclave between the Burgundian territories of Artois, Flanders and Hainault. It was important for Burgundy that the episcopal ruler of Tournai was friendly, and this had been the case in the late thirteenth and early fourteenth centuries. France also thought this see of strategic importance. So, when the bishop died in June 1433, Philip the Good's attempt to place his candidate Jehan Chevrot, president of his council, was challenged by Charles VIII's of France's intervention with Pope Eugenius IV to bestow the appointment on Jehan d'Harcourt. Philip ordered his subjects and officials to refuse to obey d'Harcourt, sent an embassy to the pope and also mustered support from Ghent and other Flemish cities. In 1435, Jehan d'Harcourt took up residence in the see but Philip had control over part of its revenues and was able eventually to persuade Eugenius to reverse his appointment and install Jehan Chevrot in the episcopate in 1436. Jehan d'Harcourt rejected this decision and Charles VII ordered the consuls of Tournai to disobey the pope. It was only when Philip the Good ordered a successful commercial boycott of Tournai that the city attempted to negotiate a settlement in 1438. A settlement in favour of Jehan Chevrot was achieved through the intervention of the Duchess Isabel and the duke of Bourbon in 1438.

When Eugenius was succeeded in February 1447 by Nicholas V, Burgundy's close relations with the Roman papacy were not disturbed. In the ensuing years, Nicholas confirmed the terms of Eugenius's concordats, gave yet more patronage to the Duchess Isabel and appointments to a further 112 livings to

Philip himself; he also provided places for the children of their officials, even granting a cardinal's hat to Jehan Rolin, son of Philip's chancellor. In 1450, Nicholas had ordered a jubilee year during which all Christians were required to make a pilgrimage to the eternal city of Rome on pain of excommunication, unless they paid for an indulgence not to do so. Nicholas retrospectively granted an indulgence to the duke and any of Philip's subjects who had not made this pilgrimage so long as they made seven visits to the seven churches at Malines. This was an important concession, not only because it saved Philip and his subjects considerable expense and inconvenience, but also because it boosted the economy of Malines. Philip maintained this relationship under successive popes, bolstered by his personal enthusiasm for the crusading ventures of popes Callixtus III and Pius II.

The kingdoms of England, France and Spain, the expansionist dukedom of Burgundy and the German-speaking principalities of the Holy Roman Empire were all caught up in this diplomatic game. The changing alliances and frictions between these players meant that first one and then another had influence over the papacy and hence over aspects of its own territorial church.

Returning to the question of sovereignty within the state, it is important to observe that the concessions that monarchs won from popes were valuable but they did not always mean that kings and dukes controlled their territorial churches. Philip of Burgundy was able to place his servants and relatives in sees and archbishoprics, but this did not mean that his rule ran within them. By the early fifteenth century, the influence of Burgundy in the city of Liège seemed secure, as the secular power of the bishop of Liège seemed minimal and the influence of the emperor negligible. Yet Bishop Jehan de Heinsberg managed to maintain his authority over that city from 1419 to 1455 and even to wage war on Philip the Good briefly in 1430. Philip the Good achieved what seemed to be a humiliating defeat of de Heinsberg in 1431 and an apparently one-sided treaty of alliance in 1434, but events were to show that the bishop of Liège was not prepared to kowtow to Burgundy. Philip and his successor had, as we have seen above, to mount successive campaigns against the city before they were able to achieve control.

Above all, rulers were concerned to control appointments to benefices (especially bishoprics and archbishoprics) and, thereby, arbitration in disputes and the extent of papal taxation. This was true in all three 'states' under discussion. We have already seen that this was the case in Burgundy and in England (both of which had reached a concordat with Pope Martin V in 1418). Such issues were central to the official English break with Rome in the 1530s. Charles VII of France submitted to Pope Martin V in 1426 but demanded the right to appoint to 500 benefices. In 1438, the Pragmatic Sanction of Bourges limited papal control inside France. Significantly, the French king resisted papal pressure to end this and allow visits from papal legates in 1440–42 and 1452. The situation in France demonstrates that it was not a simple two-way struggle for control between ruler and papacy, however. The king would lean on papal support when it suited him, for example when he wanted to collect clerical tenths in 1447 and 1457. Others were intervening to assert ecclesiastical patronage. The duke of Brittany, probably the most powerful and independent of the French princes apart from Burgundy, made his own concordat (of Redon) with the pope in 1441, whereby Duke Jean obtained a concession that only bishops loyal to him would be appointed to Breton dioceses.

Secular rulers were sometimes so in need of the support of the territorial church that they seem to have surrendered their hard-won control over it. A possible interpretation of events in France is that, during the Hundred Years War with England, the Valois monarchs of France, in order to secure financial and other kinds of support for their cause, were forced to make concessions to the first estate of the clergy at the assemblies known as estates general that gathered to discuss affairs of the kingdom. Leading churchmen were also allowed by the king to meet at synods to discuss collective ecclesiastical strategy. In this way the French monarchs permitted the French church to build the traditions and institutions of a 'national' 'Gallican' church. Thus churchmen were able to negotiate on their own terms, not only with the pope, but also with the French sovereign, and they were able to exploit the European diplomatic situation to achieve their own ends. The so-called Pragmatic Sanction of Bourges (1438) limited both papal and monarchical control over the church in France.

However, Louis XI abolished the Pragmatic Sanction in 1461 and reached a concordat with the pope in 1472, whereby he and the pope divided up ecclesiastical appointments between them. The pope reserved some appointments for the king's nominees and agreed to appoint to others (for example, sees) only with the king's consent. Louis seems only to have observed this concordat when it suited his interests and used the threat of the restoration of the Pragmatic Sanction to put pressure on Pope Sixtus IV. For example, he submitted the concordat for approval to the Parlement of Paris in 1475, at a time when he suspected Sixtus of favouring the interests of Charles the Bold of Burgundy. Louis is said to have had a bench of bishops who were amenable to his wishes. After Louis's death there seems to have been a Gallican reaction and a call for the restitution of the Pragmatic Sanction. The regency government of Charles VIII did not restore the Pragmatic Sanction, however, and had a working relationship with the papacy.

The royal parlements gained considerable experience in dealing with cases arising from disputed benefices, and made far-reaching claims for royal jurisdiction (sometimes in opposition to what the monarch actually wanted to do!). Unsurprisingly, they were to be found among the strongest supporters of the Pragmatic Sanction. By the end of Louis XI's reign, most of the bishops appear to have opposed the Pragmatic Sanction. It does seem, however, that the position of churchmen vis-à-vis the sanction was perhaps dependent on self-interest (Lewis, 1968, pp. 319–24).

EXERCISE

Why do you think secular rulers were keen to control the church in their territories?

This is a matter of interpretation. Re-read the above account if you are uncertain. Try to answer the question in just a few lines. Note down which example you would use to support each point.

Spend about 20 minutes on this exercise.

SPECIMEN ANSWER

- The church was rich and monarchs, especially those involved in foreign or civil wars, needed money to finance their activities. They wanted to levy taxes on the church. The papacy could also confer lucrative rights on the localities. For example, the pope granted Malines a long-term right to the pilgrimages of Burgundians who did not travel to Rome for the papal jubilee year of 1550. This brought great prosperity to the churches and the town.

- Appointing crown servants or relatives to ecclesiastical positions, paid from church revenues, was a cheap way of paying for loyal service to the sovereign and of supporting illegitimate children and other dependent relatives. For example, Philip the Good obtained a see for his illegitimate half-brother Jehan and his own illegitimate son David.

- Monarchs were not keen to see foreign influence in their kingdoms, dukedoms or principalities. (Concordats between France and the papacy and Burgundy and the papacy limited this influence and restricted appeals from these territories to Rome. Statutes of Praemunire that forbade judicial appeals outside England to the papal curia indicated similar motivation. During the early years of the English Reformation, such statutes were enforced.) When the papacy was being heavily influenced by another power, papal interference was especially detested.

- Sovereigns also wished to shape the beliefs, morals and behaviour of their subjects. For example, religious belief was not considered to be a private matter.

Summary

Catholics were divided when it came to identifying the location of sovereignty within the church – was it located in the papacy or in the general councils? Monarchs also participated in this debate and were, in addition, torn between their deep commitment to Catholicism and spiritual authority, on the one hand, and their own temporal ambitions, on the other.

CONCLUSION

Western Christians shared a core set of beliefs. They also shared a conviction that uniformity of belief was essential. This said, far from being a single set of beliefs that transcended state boundaries and unified people, Catholic culture embraced many national, regional and local differences, a very few of which we have been able to study here. Christians, lay and ecclesiastical, high and low, argued about the location of sovereignty in the church – did ultimate authority lie with Scripture (the Bible), the papacy or the general councils? To what extent was it acceptable for the papacy to intervene in the affairs of temporal states? We have also considered the types of sources and techniques for their analysis that historians are able to use as a way into these subjects.

Now you will be able to discuss:

- to what extent Christians belonged to a unified belief system
- who was sovereign in the Catholic Church
- why and how individual states fought for control over the Catholic Church in and near their territories
- how historians can use the architecture, art and artefacts associated with a place of public worship to deepen our understanding of mainstream religious belief and worship.

REFERENCES

British Library Cotton Julius E.iv. *Pageant of the Birth, Life and Death of Richard de Beauchamp, Earl of Warwick*.

de Stavelot, J. (1861) *Chronique, 1440–1449*, ed. A. Borgnet, Brussels, CRH.

Labarge, M.W. (2005) *Medieval Travellers: The Rich and Restless*, London, Phoenix.

Leff, G. (1967) *Heresy in the Later Middle Ages: The Relation of Heterodoxy to Dissent c 1250 – c 1450*, 2 vols, Manchester, Manchester University Press.

Lewis, P.S. (1968) *Later Medieval France: The Polity*, London, Macmillan.

McSheffrey, S and Tanner, N. (eds) (2003) *Lollards of Coventry, 1486–1522*, Camden Fifth Series, vol. 23, Cambridge, Cambridge University Press.

Vaughan, R. (2002) *Philip the Good*, London, Boydell.

van der Velden, H. (2000) *The Donor's Image. Gerard Loyet and the Votive Portraits of Charles the Bold*, Burgundica II, Turnhout, Brepols.

FURTHER READING

Unit 1

Avril, F. (ed.) (2003) *Jean Fouquet, Peintre et enlumineur du XVe siècle*: Paris, Bibliothèque nationale de France, Hazan.

Leroy Ladurie, E. (1987) *The French Royal State* (trans. J. Vale), Oxford, Blackwell.

Taylor, C.D. (2006) *Joan of Arc: la Pucelle*, Manchester, Manchester University Press.

Unit 2

Small, G. (1997) *George Chastelain and the Shaping of Valois Burgundy: Political and Historical Culture at Court in the Fifteenth Century*, London, Royal Historical Society/Woodbridge, Boydell & Brewer.

Boulton, D'A. and Veenstra, J. (ed.) (2006) *The Ideology of Burgundy. The Promotion of National Consciousness*, 1364–1565, Leyden, Brill.

Unit 3

Carpenter, C. (1980) 'The Beauchamp affinity: a study of bastard feudalism at work', *English Historical Review*, vol. 95, pp. 514–32.

Cook, David R. (1984) *Lancastrians and Yorkists: The Wars of the Roses*, London, Longman.

Davis, N. (ed.) (2004) *Paston Letters and Papers of the Fifteenth Century*, 2 vols, 1971–1976, Oxford, Oxford University Press.

Dyer, C. C. (1989) *Standards of Living in the Later Middle Ages*, Cambridge, Cambridge University Press.

Gillingham, J. (1981) *Wars of the Roses,* London, Weidenfeld & Nicolson.

Hicks, M.A. (1988) *Warwick the Kingmaker*, Oxford, Oxford University Press.

Hicks, M. (1995) *Bastard Feudalism*, London, Longman.

Keen, M. (2003) *England in the Later Middle Ages*, 2nd edn, London, Routledge.

Thomson, J.A.F. (ed.) (1988) *Towns and Townspeople in the Fifteenth Century*, Gloucester.

Unit 4

Barnswell, P.S., Cross, Claire and Rycraft, Ann (2005) *Mass and Parish in Late Medieval England: The Use of York,* Reading, Spire Books.

Bossy, J. (1987) *Christianity in the West, 1400–1700*, Oxford, Oxford University Press.

Brown, A.D. (1995) *Popular Piety in Late Medieval England: The Diocese of Salisbury 1250–1550*, Oxford, Oxford University Press.

Luxton, Imogen (1971) 'The Lichfield Court Book: a postscript' on the course website.

Moore, R.I. (1985) *The Origins of European Dissent*, Oxford, Blackwell.

Rubin, M. (1991) *Corpus Christi: The Eucharist in Late Medieval Culture*, Cambridge, Cambridge University Press.

Swanson, R.N. (1995) *Religion and Devotion in Europe, c.1215 to c.1515*, Cambridge, .Cambridge University Press.

Thompson J.A.F. (1980) *Popes and Princes, 1417–1517: Politics and Polity in the Late Medieval Church*, London, Allen & Unwin.

GLOSSARY

Apostles: A select group of men commissioned by Christ to spread the Gospel. These included eleven of the original twelve disciples as well as St Paul and others.

Apostolic succession: The original commission from Christ was said to pass down to others through the laying on of hands. So the Popes received their commission directly from St Peter and passed it on to archbishops and bishops.

Aristocracy: Generally considered to be the upper class of society and to include members of the peerage and the upper gentry (especially those who are knighted).

Aquitaine: Also known as Gascony.

Bastard feudalism: A social system whereby the powerful bound men to their service for a given period in exchange for a fee, a uniform and lodging. Also known as 'good lordship' and 'livery and maintenance'.

Black Death: The waves of bubonic and pneumonic plague that swept through Europe c.1348–1349.

Cathars: Held dualist beliefs in which a good spiritual world was paralleled by a carnal, physical world of evil.

Churchwardens: Customarily the Rector or vicar of the parish selected one churchwarden and the people of the parish another on an annual basis to see to the good running of the church. Churchwardens were responsible for responding to the Bishop's and Archdeacon's visitations of the parish, for collecting dues etc. In some places women heads of household were eligible for this office. In any event the churchwardens' wives assisted their husbands.

Clergy: The first or spiritual estate. It is usually divided vertically into the secular clergy and the regular clergy.

Secular clergy: Include all archbishops, bishops, archdeacons, deans, priests, deacons and subdeacons who do not belong to a monastic order. Secular clergy are also divided horizontally into the upper clergy (archbishops, bishops, archdeacons, deans) and the lower clergy (priests, deacons, subdeacons who serve as parish priests, rectors and vicars, and often as schoolmasters etc.).

Regular clergy: Include all monks, friars and nuns who follow a 'rule' such as that of St Francis or St Augustine. Regular clergy are also divided horizontally into upper clergy (abbots, priors, abbessesses and prioresses) and lower clergy (monks, friars, nuns).

Clerk: Normally used to mean an ordained priest or deacon (i.e. clerk in holy orders). Many did perform administrative duties of the type performed in modern society by minor civil servants or clerks.

Communion in both kinds: In Protestant churches at Communion both consecrated bread and wine were offered to the laity.

Communion in one kind: In the Catholic Church both consecrated bread and wine were blessed by the priest but only bread was offered to the laity.

Conciliar Movement: A fifteenth century movement to rule the Catholic Church through General Councils. It was seen as a threat by the Papacy, (Conciliarism).

Creed: A statement of belief. Taken from the Latin for 'I believe'.

Crusades: Holy wars were chiefly a feature of the thirteenth century but still occurring in the fourteenth and fifteenth centuries. They focussed on repossession of the sacred sites in Jerusalem. Crusades were, however, also used to extirpate heresies (e.g. in 1487 against the Waldenses).

Deference: In a hierarchical society individuals deferred to those above them in the hierarchy. Within the family wives deferred to husbands; children to parents, sisters to brothers.

Demography: Study of population.

Deposition: Removal of the monarch from the throne e.g. Edward IV in 1470. The term deposition is also used to mean the testimony of a witness in court.

Diocese: The Church was divided into dioceses. Each diocese was made up of a number of parishes. A Bishop headed each diocese and provided pastoral care and discipline. He was aided in this work by Archdeacons and Rural Deans. Although his seat was the cathedral, the cathedral was governed by a Dean and Chapter.

Family, extended: Mostly used by historians to mean the entire family, co-resident or not, including grandparents, parents, uncles, aunts, cousins adult offspring and children. Sometimes also referred to as the 'wider family'.

Family, nuclear: Parents and children who are co-resident.

Formulary: A book containing appropriate forms of words for wills, bonds etc.

Gascony: Also known as Aquitaine.

Good works: Included good deeds but also encompassed such things as the endowment of masses and the performance of pilgrimages.

Great Schism: Between 1303 and 1378 there was a pope in Avignon, France (Clement V, John XXII, Clement VI, Urban V and Gregory XI) who was, in effect, a puppet of the French kings. Then, after the election of Urban VI as pope in Rome and the election of Pope Clement VII as pope in Avignon, Catholic Christendom was split into two until 1417, in what came to be called The Great Schism.

Guild or Gild: An association or fraternity. Some were trade associations which, among other things, regulated trading practices and personnel, provided support for the widows and children of members etc. Others were religious associations.

Heiress: In the event of no male issue (son, son's son etc), freehold lands were inherited by the surviving daughter(s) of the landowner. If there were more than one daughter (as in the case of the Earl of Warwick) the daughters became co-heiresses and inherited equally.

Henry VI: 1st reign of 1437–1461. Readeption of 1470–1471, the period when Henry VI was restored to throne by the Earl of Warwick

Heresy: A belief or beliefs that went against those approved by the Church authorities.

Indulgences: An individual could be granted an indulgence for absolution from sins committed on performance of a 'good work'. Eventually this practice was abused and indulgences were granted in straight exchange for money. This constituted simony.

Inquisition: A special ecclesiastical court set up by a Pope or Bishop to try supposed heretics.

Jubilee Year: From time to time the Popes would declare a Jubilee Year. If an individual made a pilgrimage to Rome during this year, he or she would earn indulgences which they could use to absolve themselves from sins committed without the need for penance.

Justices of the Peace: An ancient county office that by 1320 had become an established part of local government. Justices supervised the work of surveyors and others; they also had criminal jurisdiction in certain respects (and referred other cases to the Assize courts) and administrative duties.

Laity: People who were not clergy.

Legitimate: A child born within marriage. The English placed a good deal of importance on legitimate descent. Titles and land were passed through legitimate heirs and heiresses.

Liturgy: Forms of public religious service.

Livery: A badged uniform.

Low Countries: What are today Belgium and the Netherlands.

Minor: An individual who had not yet come of age.

Papal Curia: Court.

Parish: England was divided into parishes for convenience. Each parish was under the care (cure) of a curate, who was an ordained clergyman (priest). Depending on how he received his income, this priest was known as the rector or vicar. The word 'curate' came to be used for assistants only.

Parliament: A body of two Houses (Lords and Commons) called intermittently by the King to grant subsidies and taxes. Boroughs (towns with a borough charter) and Shires (counties) had representation. Originally the chief business of the English Parliament had been judicial (e.g. cases of treason) but this was changing fast. The need for money to fight the war strengthened Parliament's hand *vis à vis* the monarchy. Parliamentary consent was not required to pass legislation (laws or statutes of the realm) but Kings found it convenient to declare laws in the presence of Parliament.

Peasants Revolt, 1381: English revolt against the Poll Tax, led by Jack Straw and Wat Tyler. Quashed peaceably by young king Richard II with very few of the rebels being executed.

Pilgrimage: A visit to a shrine or shrines performed as a 'good work' or as a penance for sins the individual had committed, in order to earn absolution or forgiveness.

Poll Tax, 1379: Graduated tax on individuals. This acknowledged changes in society consequent upon the growth of towns and non agricultural occupations by providing a scale of equivalencies whereby, for example, lawyers and merchants could be equated with knights and esquires.

Preamble: The opening paragraph of a will and testament in which the testator bequeathes his soul.

Purgatory: A place of waiting for the souls of the deceased who could not be admitted to heaven immediately because they had not been absolved of all their sins. The time in purgatory could be shortened if masses were said on earth for them.

Retainers: Under feudalism retainers were the armed men kept by individual lords and knights; under bastard feudalism few lords kept armed retainers; rather, they could call upon particular men for any kind of service whenever there was a need.

Sacraments: The Catholic Church maintained that there were seven sacraments or outward signs of an inward, invisible grace. These were Baptism, Confirmation, Marriage, Holy Orders, Penance, Communion, Holy Unction (the last rites). Protestant churches rejected most of these, generally retaining only baptism and communion.

Sepulchre: Tomb.

Shrine: A holy place erected to commemorate a saint or Jesus Christ. There would normally be an altar and a reliquary (containing some part of the saint).

Statute of Labourers: 1351, English Act of Parliament which set wages and prices at pre-plague levels and strove to tie labourers to the land (serfdom).

Sumptuary laws: passed by King Edward III regulated the types and colour of clothing that could be worn by various sections of society.

Testator: The individual who made a will.

Three Estates: Clergy, Nobility, People.

Trading Monopolies: Exclusive rights to trade in or through a particular port or region.

Trinity: The division of the Godhead into three equal parts: God the Father, God the Son and God the Holy Spirit or Ghost.

Votive: Gift made at a shrine.

Waldensian Heresy: Medieval heresy that began in Lyons. It was characterised by a reliance on vernacular scriptures, and puritanical and pacific teachings.

INDEX